Dermatology

A SCOPE® PUBLICATION

SAMUEL M. BLUEFARB, MD
Department of Dermatology
Northwestern University, The Medical School
Chicago, Illinois

Upjohn

Library of Congress Card Number 75-112746

ISBN 0-89501-004-6

8801-07R3

Table of Contents

Introduction

The aim of this text is to correlate and supplement lectures given to students beginning the study of dermatology. The time available in the average medical school curriculum is inadequate to cover all dermatologic entities. Our purpose is not to merely publish another text on dermatology, as there are many excellent textbooks available. Rather, we hope to stimulate and arouse the interest of the student in "Concepts of Dermatology." Not only are the common dermatologic entities discussed and illustrated, but also some of the rare diseases if they illustrate a principle.

The most definitive classification is by etiology. Unfortunately, etiology is unknown in many skin diseases. Another method of classification is pathogenetic mechanisms. It rapidly becomes apparent that this doesn't work well, because in some cases the pathogenetic mechanism is not well understood and some apparently similar mechanisms cause different reaction patterns. The chapters used in this monograph are based upon *reaction patterns*. This permits differential diagnosis of "similar looking" lesions. Where applicable, the pathologic reaction pattern has been correlated with the morphologic reaction pattern. In some cases this could not be done. The papulosquamous eruptions are classified according to the morphologic reaction pattern, whereas the vesiculobullous lesions are classified according to the pathological reaction pattern.

Concepts of dermatologic diseases essentially comprise three parts: *First*, the reaction pattern, which consists of two principles, namely, (a) the stage of morphology, which is the identification of the characteristic symptoms and signs, and (b) the pathologic changes that are responsible for the clinically observed features; *second*, the stage concerned with disease mechanisms and why the particular signs and symptoms alter physiology; and *third*, the determination of predisposing and precipitating factors.

Our mission will be accomplished if this syllabus acts as a gadfly to the student to increase his interest in and desire to learn dermatology in depth.

My thanks and gratitude to my colleagues who helped in the planning and preparation of this monograph: Drs. J. Hasegara, R. Freinkel, W. Caro, and F. Levit.

Samuel M. Bluefarb, MD
Professor, Department of Dermatology
Northwestern University
The Medical School, Chicago, Illinois

Dermatitis

Dermatitis (eczema) is inflammation of the skin and one of the commonest reactions occurring in the skin. Dermatitis is the cutaneous pattern to many causative agents.

REACTION PATTERN: The reaction pattern will depend on the stage of reaction and the severity of the injury.

In the acute stage there is redness (vasodilatation of the subpapillary plexus); itching, with release of proteases and/or peptase and/or histamine; moist surface, vesicles and bullae (increase in epidermal fluid either as fluid loculi or intercellular edema [spongiosis]).

In the chronic stage there is dryness, scaling, thickening of the skin (hyperkeratosis and parakeratosis) and lichenification (acanthosis and hyperkeratosis).

CONTACT DERMATITIS

The inciting agents in contact dermatitis are externally applied and may provoke a primary irritation reaction (nonspecific) or an allergic delayed-type hypersensitivity reaction (specific). In the latter, specifically sensitized lymphocytes must be present in the circulating fluid.

Nonspecific reaction: Physiologically, the stratum corneum, especially the lower third and possibly the granular cell layer, constitutes a barrier against the ingress of most substances. A variety of chemicals, fat solvents, surface active agents, alkali, and even hot water may act to disrupt the barrier property. Xylol or turpentine applied topically, for example, may be expected to disrupt the physiological barrier and thus produce an inflammatory response of the skin in almost all individuals. More commonly, constant or repeated use of soaps and detergents in a variety of occupations may also result in inflammation. In this situation, the action may not be a direct chemical disruption of the physiological barrier zone but rather is secondary to the defatting of the stratum corneum. It should be recalled that the pliability and moist texture of the skin surface are dependent, to a large extent, upon the complex hydrophilic mixture of lipids in the stratum corneum and that constant removal of this lipid material removes the ability of the stratum corneum to retain water. A thoroughly defatted stratum corneum, therefore, may be expected to scale, flake, and fissure, and become ineffective as a barrier.

Specific reaction: In contrast to the nonspecific or primary irritant forms of dermatitis, the delayed hypersensitivity type of contact dermatitis requires a second cellular factor carried to the skin by the circulation. This form of cutaneous inflammation requires a previous sensitizing exposure to the chemical, which may be as short as five days before the eruption. On this sensitizing exposure, the chemical is carried by the lymphatic channels to the lymph nodes and in certain individuals induces the proliferation of lymphocytes, which are capable of reacting specifically with the

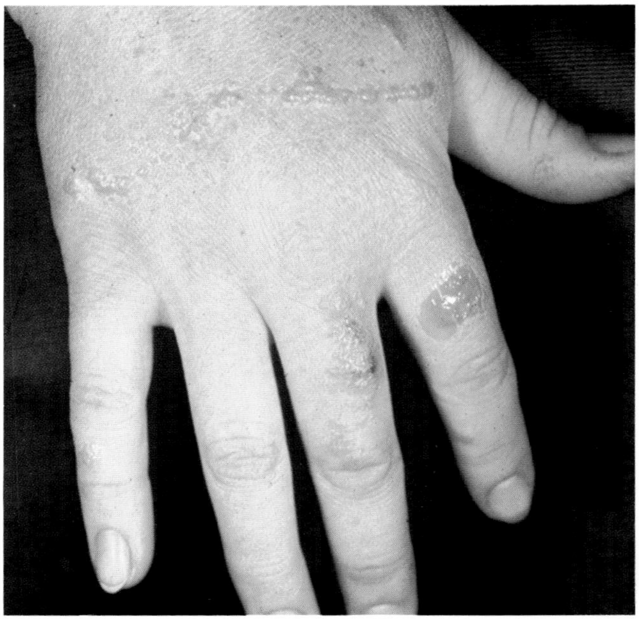

Figure 1. Linear vesicular eruption due to poison ivy

Figure 2. (top) Contact dermatitis at nape of neck due to nickel clasp
Figure 3. (middle) Contact dermatitis due to shoes

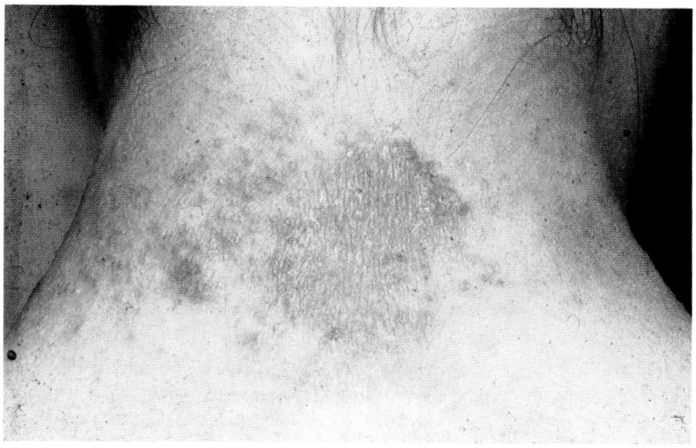

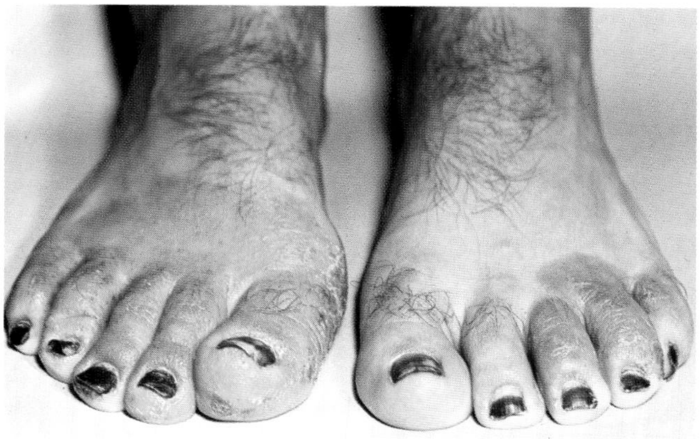

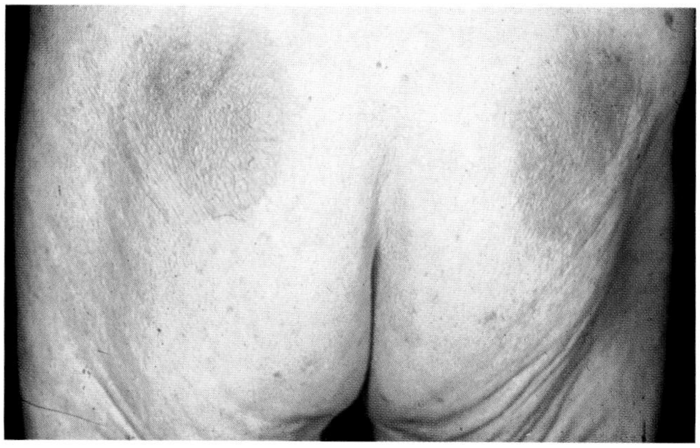

Figure 4. Contact dermatitis due to leather truss

chemical or chemical-protein molecule formed by a covalent bond. Upon reexposure or continued exposure, the chemical absorbed from the surface reacts with the sensitized lymphocytes in the subpapillary vessels, releasing a factor that changes the surface properties of other mononuclear cells and the endothelium. The mononuclear cells then adhere to the endothelium and migrate through the vessel wall to the surrounding tissue. Lysosomal enzymes released in this process are thought to provoke the inflammation of dermatitis.

"ATOPIC" DERMATITIS

The basic problem appears to be a (genetically conferred) hyperirritable skin detectable as variable degrees of dryness (xerosis), a tendency toward an exaggerated lichenification, white dermographism, delayed blanch phenomenon, and a low itch threshold. This hyperirritable skin is usually inherited in association with atopy

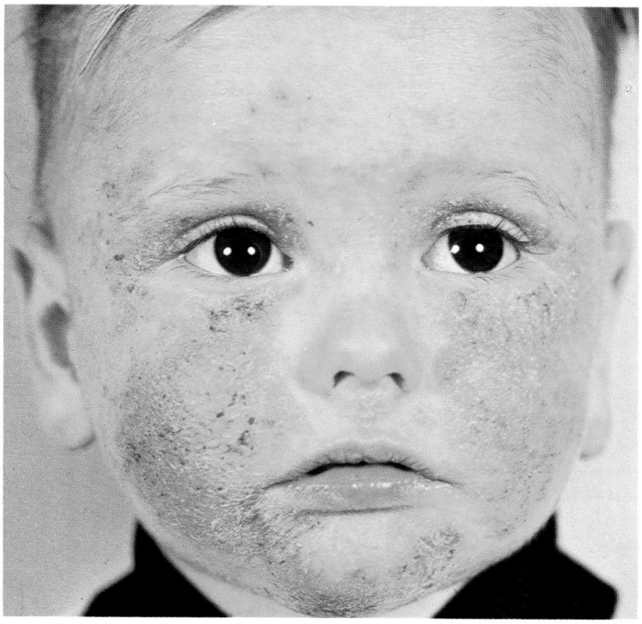

Figure 5. Atopic dermatitis

– hay fever, asthma, or urticaria – but the cutaneous manifestations of the disease apparently are not dependent upon circulating antibodies. The low itch threshold triggers rubbing or scratching, producing lichenification. This, in turn, is associated with still a lower itch threshold for a multitude of inciting agents that would not provoke a dermatitis in the average skin. The reason for the localization of the lesions in the flexural areas – face, neck, cubital and popliteal fossae, and hands – is not known. Patients with atopic dermatitis are prone to acquire bacterial and virus infections.

Figure 6. Lichen simplex chronicus on leg

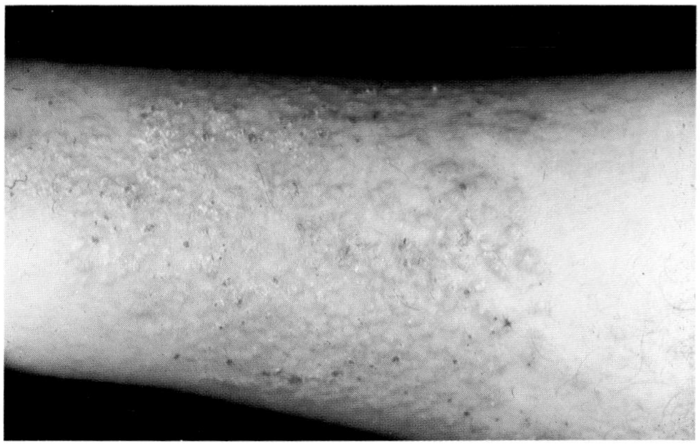

LICHEN SIMPLEX CHRONICUS

The mechanism of itching, scratching, lichenification, and lowering of the itch threshold appears to be operative in the genesis of this disorder. The other abnormalities – white dermographism, delayed blanch phenomenon, and atopy – are not necessarily present. Although the lesions are most common around the neck, they may occur on any part of the body.

SEBORRHEIC DERMATITIS

Dermatitis localizing in the seborrheic areas – the face, especially the nasolabial folds, and eyebrows; retroauricular areas; sternal areas; interscapular areas; and the scalp – usually presents scaling with minimal lichenification. However, the eruption can become acute, either independently or in association with bacterial overgrowth. This form of dermatitis may occur concomitantly with acne, rosacea, or psoriasis.

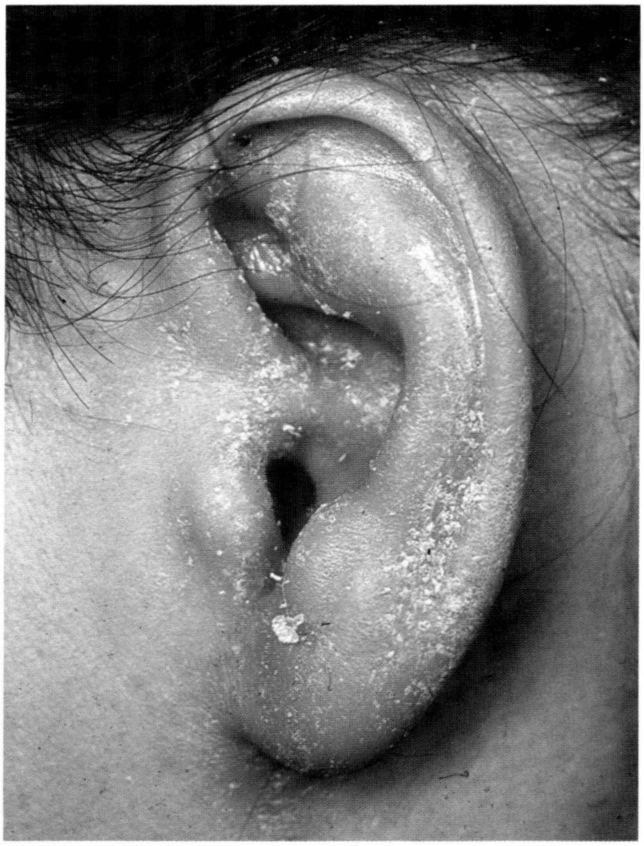

Figure 7. Seborrheic dermatitis

INFECTIOUS ECZEMATOID DERMATITIS

Occasionally, a bacterial pustular infection, such as a chronic middle-ear infection, will provoke the reaction of dermatitis on the skin that is exposed to pustular drainage. This inflammatory reaction to the products of an infectious process is called infectious eczematoid dermatitis. It should be noted that the skin will also have an altered but abundant flora of microorganisms. Thus any acute dermatitis may have a bacterial component as one of the irritants. The clinician must determine whether the bacterial infection is the primary cause of the eruption or merely a secondary overgrowth in the presence of dermatitis.

NUMMULAR DERMATITIS

Nummular dermatitis is essentially a morphologic diagnosis and simply means coin-shaped dermatitis. Often this form of dermatitides is observed with a nummular morphology on xerotic skin. Occasionally, nummular lesions may occur (over much of the cutaneous surface) as eruptions secondary to localized acute dermatitis. Infrequently, disseminated nummular lesions appear without apparent cause. In many of these eruptions the bacterial component of the dermatitis appears to be a major factor. It has been speculated that the initial lesions are focal bacterial infections, with secondary inflammation to the products of the infection in a circle around the focal point.

STASIS DERMATITIS

A variety of factors may lead to discoloration, fibrosis, and ulceration of the skin of the legs, following minor trauma. The commonest factor is lymphedema secondary to venous insufficiency. However, repeated trauma, purpura, thrombophlebitis, and prolonged nonspecific dermatitis around the malleolar area can end in pigmented hemosiderotic, taut, abnormal skin, which becomes a locus minoris resistentia that is susceptible to dermatitic reaction to a great number of nonspecific irritants.

INFANTILE ECZEMA

Dermatitis in infants frequently is not morphologically diagnostic. Lichenification of the skin usually does not appear in the first year or two of life. The eruption tends

Figure 8. (top) Infectious eczematoid dermatitis of breasts

Figure 9. (middle) Nummular dermatitis

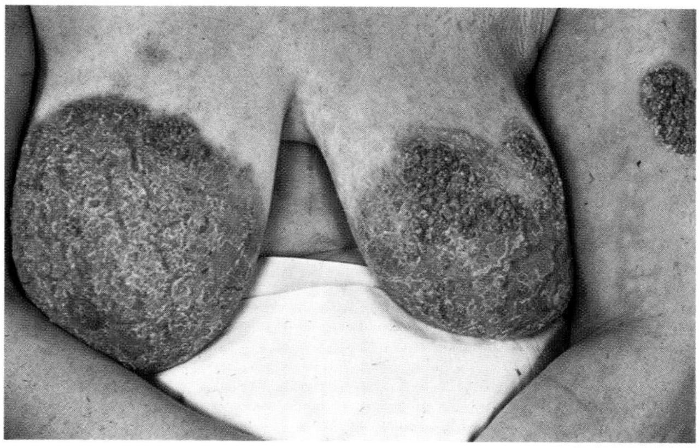

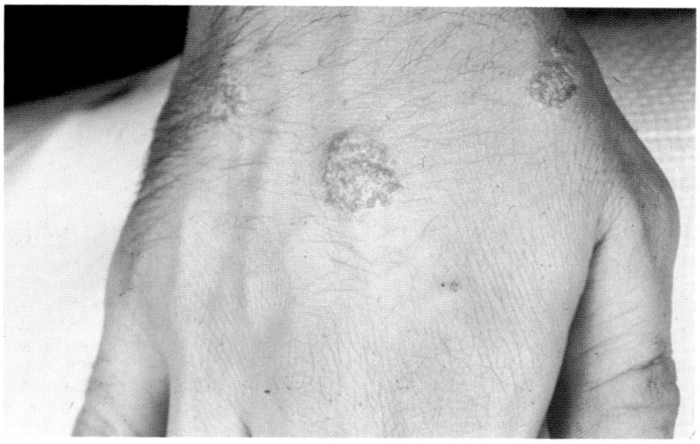

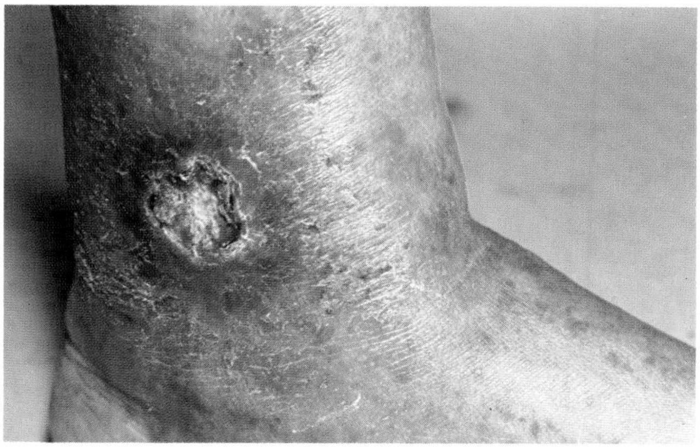

Figure 10. Stasis dermatitis with ulcer

to be acute or subacute in appearance. Infantile eczema may be a manifestation of contact dermatitis, seborrheic dermatitis, or atopic dermatitis.

EXFOLIATIVE DERMATITIS

Any reaction of dermatitis affecting the entire cutaneous surface is termed exfoliative dermatitis or erythroderma. The inciting agents of this condition are multiform. The exfoliative dermatitis may be the aggravated stages of atopic dermatitis, psoriasis, seborrheic dermatitis, or contact dermatitis, or one of the other less-common cutaneous diseases. Alternatively, it may be a manifestation of some systemic disease, particularly the lymphomas and neoplasms. The patient with exfoliative dermatitis has serious impairment of the functions of the skin. There is inability to tolerate temperature variations, and the patient is constantly shivering or bundled under bedcovers. There is significant protein loss. A folic acid deficiency may also become evident. With the disruption of the cutaneous barrier, the patient is prone to bacterial and viral infections, and excessive sweating may result. In a significant percentage of patients, no demonstrable primary cutaneous or systemic disease can be detected.

In other inflammatory reactions, all the necessary inciting agents are carried to the skin by the circulation. Examples of this are drug eruptions, and for most drug eruptions the exact mechanism of the inflammatory eruption has not been defined. It has been classified as an allergic reaction without satisfactory demonstration of allergy or is classified noncommittally as drug idiosyncrasy. The severity of the inflammation ranges from simple erythema or urticaria to massive destruction of tissues. In some cases, the inflammation is sufficiently mild to fall within the clinical morphologic classification of dermatitis.

The inciting agent may reach the epidermis via the circulation. Unknown agents apparently reach the

Figure 11. Exfoliative dermatitis

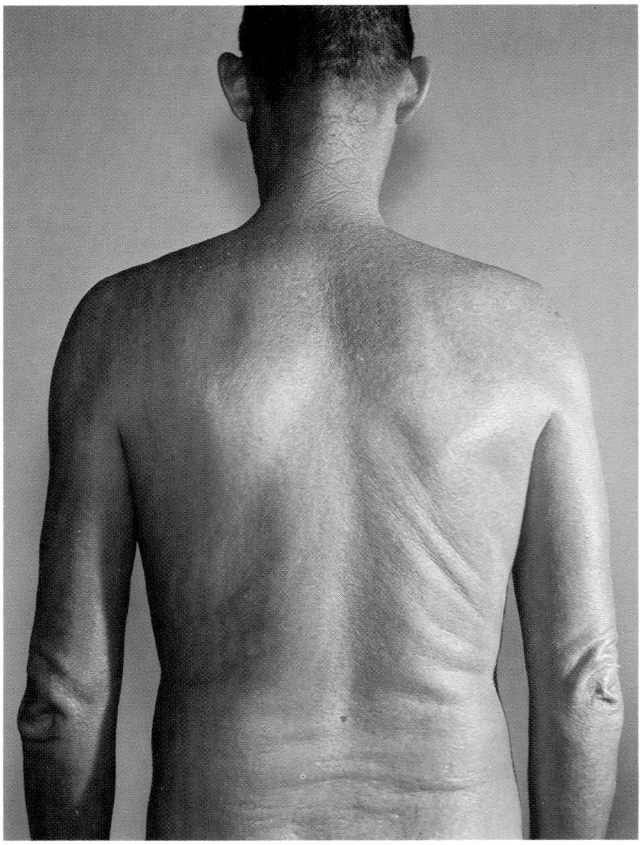

epidermis in neoplastic diseases under certain circumstances and produce dermatitis. The relationship of some conditions of exfoliative dermatitis and lymphomas is well known.

In certain situations there may be congenital abnormalities of the epidermis that tend to produce a dermatitis. An example is congenital ichthyosiform erythroderma and phenylketonuria. Other cases would include the macrocytic anemias, vascular diseases, Aldrich syndrome, and degenerative or aging processes.

Papulosquamous Eruptions

The papulosquamous eruptions are a heterogenous group of diseases. Three of these have distinctive morphological features and can usually be diagnosed clinically and verified by histopathology; these are pityriasis rosea, psoriasis, and lichen planus. The etiology of these eruptions is not completely understood. Some of the others – secondary syphilis, tinea circinata, seborrheic dermatitis, and other forms such as parapsoriasis – are unrelated diseases that may simulate the papulosquamous eruptions morphologically. Note that the raised lesions in the papulosquamous eruptions are produced by an increase in the thickness of the epidermis, whereas the raised lesions in the reaction pattern are smooth nodules produced by space-consuming pathologic processes in the dermis.

REACTION PATTERNS: Redness (erythema), raised lesions (papules), and scales.

Gross morphology: Inflammatory reactions similar to those of chronic dermatitis occur in a variety of cutaneous diseases. All of these have some degree of scaling and thickening of the epidermis. The scales may be minimal or so abundant that the floor literally will be covered like a blanket of snow. Alternatively, self-treatment by the patient may have removed almost all of the scales so that this morphologic feature may not be apparent.

Microscopic morphology: Thickening of the epidermis (acanthosis) is almost always present in various forms. Psoriasis is associated with an increased mitotic activity. Hyperkeratosis, with or without parakeratosis, is found even in the absence of gross scaling. The dermis usually has mononuclear cell infiltration, which may be perivascular and periappendageal or uniformly distributed in a band in the upper dermis.

PSORIASIS

This is a heritable disease which manifests itself as a morphologically distinct lesion. Characteristically, the psoriatic papule has thick imbricated scales extending almost to the edge but usually leaving a rim of dusky-red base. The papule or plaque is sharply outlined; i.e., the transition from affected to unaffected skin is abrupt. Removal of the scales may reveal multiple punctate bleeding points (Auspitz sign). Lesions frequently appear on the scalp, extensor surfaces of the extremities, the trunk, and the nails. The fingernail changes – simple pitting of the nail surface or ragged opacities of the distal ends of the nails – are frequently seen and represent disturbances in keratinization of the nail plate or the distal ends of the nail bed. In some patients the synovial

Figure 12. (top) Psoriasis

Figure 13. (bottom) Psoriasis

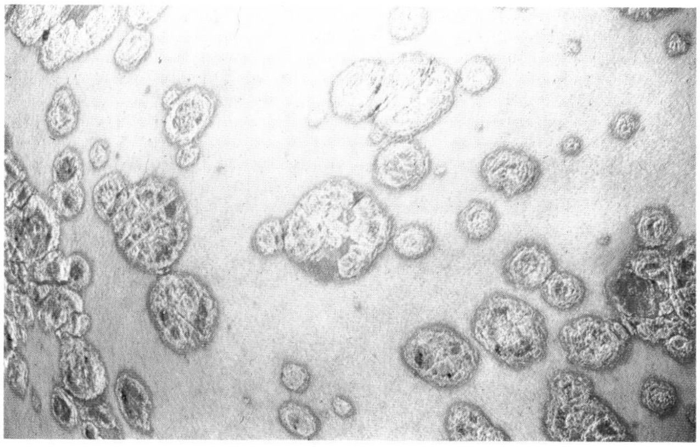

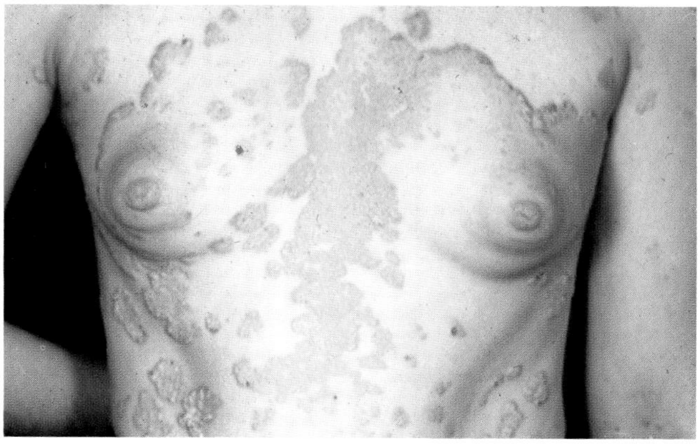

membranes and, secondarily, the adjacent bones may become inflamed. It is important from a therapeutic point of view to differentiate true psoriatic arthritis from rheumatoid and gouty arthritis.

Microscopically, the psoriatic lesion shows an alternating hyperkeratosis and parakeratosis, thinning of the suprapapillary epidermis, and club-like acanthosis of the rete ridges. The papillae of the dermis are enlarged, and the capillaries of the papillae are tortuous and dilated. There is an acceleration of epidermal metabolism almost as if the skin were unable to stop the increased metabolism of the injured epidermis. Frequently, psoriatic lesions appear following trauma or inflammation (Koebner phenomenon).

LICHEN PLANUS

This is a disease of unknown origin but with a characteristic morphology. The papules of lichen planus have minimal scales. They are angular, violaceous, and flat-topped with a tendency to retain their outline as a unit even when the papules coalesce to form plaques. The surface appears shiny, probably due to light reflection from a uniform thickening of the granular cell layer. The redness has a bluish cast which may be related to the band-like infiltrate in the upper dermis. A lace-like appearance of the surface (Wickham striae) can be demonstrated best by partial clearing with light mineral oil or other organic clearing agents. Itching is usually severe. Mucosal involvement may occur in the form of white interlacing lines or patches. The lesions appear most frequently on the flexural surfaces of the extremities, buccal mucosa, and the genitalia.

Microscopically, there is hyperkeratosis, thickening of the granular cell layer, saw-toothed acanthosis, liquefaction degeneration of the basal cell layer, and a band-like round cell infiltrate in the upper dermis hugging the dermoepidermal junction. The ingestion of various chemicals such as arsphenamine, gold, Ata-

Figure 14. (top) Pitting of nails associated with psoriasis

Figure 15. (middle) Lichen planus, forearm

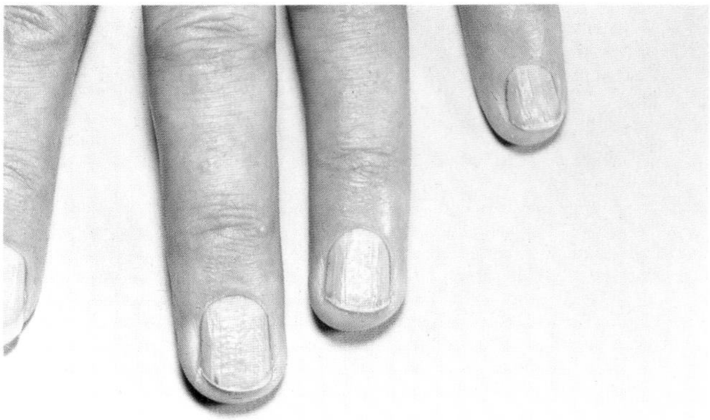

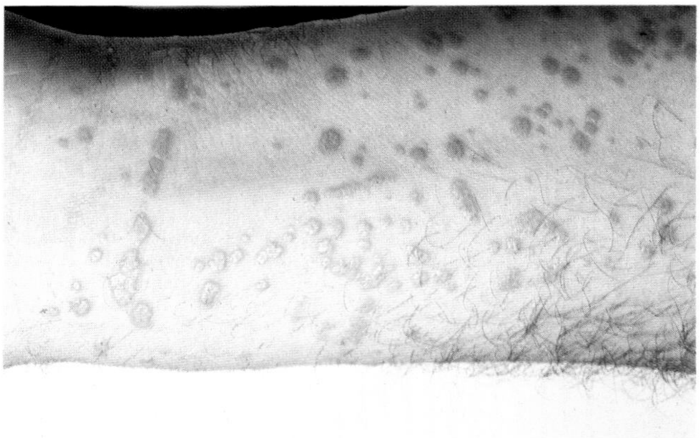

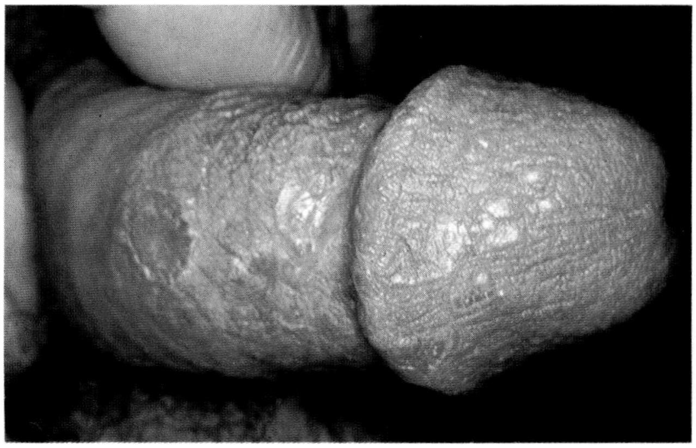

Figure 16. Lichen planus

brine, daptazole, thiazides, as well as contact with color developer chemicals have been associated with the eruption of lichen planus. Para-aminosalicylic acid, chemically related to color developers, has caused lichenoid eruptions. However, the vast majority of lichenoid eruptions occur with no demonstrable inciting agents. Lichen planus is probably a systemic disorder.

PITYRIASIS ROSEA

The duration of this eruption is usually 4 to 6 weeks, with the characteristic morphology consisting of finely scaling ovoid lesions with the long axis parallel to Langer lines. The eruption is usually bilateral and symmetrical. It may be preceded by a single scaling lesion (herald patch) which may be mistaken for tinea circinata. There are no known sequelae to this disease and the lesions occur only once. If the lesions occur repeatedly or persist beyond 2 or 3 months, the patient may be found to have a pityriasis rosea-like drug eruption or lichen planus.

MISCELLANEOUS ERUPTIONS

Three infrequently encountered diseases may simulate the lesion of psoriasis and should be kept in mind in atypical psoriatic eruptions. These are mycosis fungoides, pityriasis rubra pilaris, and parapsoriasis. Mycosis fungoides is a lymphoma that remains localized in the cutaneous tissues for long periods of time. In the typical patient, the initial stage of the lesion is a nonhealing chronic dermatitis. This is followed by a plaque formation mimicking the psoriatic plaque. The final stage is the formation of tumors and ulcerations.

Pityriasis rubra pilaris may occur as a palmar scaling and erythema, with a sharp line of demarcation at the junction of the affected and unaffected skin along the lateral aspects of the fingers and the thenar and hypothenar skin. Similar-type lesions may affect the soles of the feet. Follicular keratotic lesions on the dorsal

Figure 17. Pityriasis rosea with large herald patch

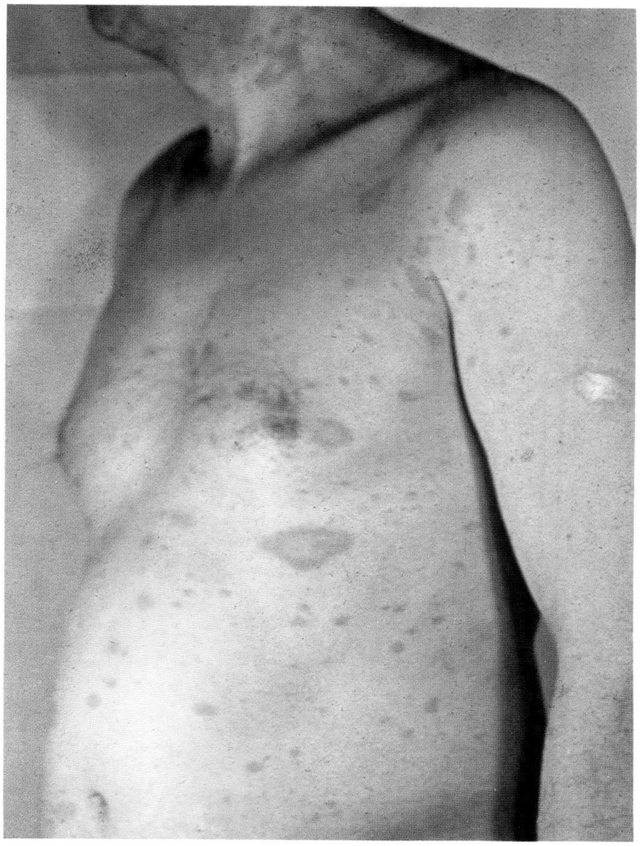

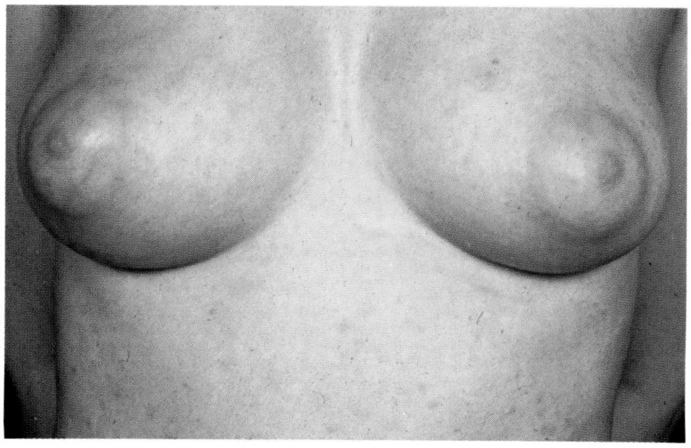

Figure 18. Parapsoriasis

aspects of the proximal phalanges, knees, or elbows may be present.

Parapsoriasis is a heterogeneous group of eruptions of unknown origin in which fine dust-like scaling on a light-red base occurs over extended periods of time. The eruptions are usually bilateral and symmetrical and almost always affect the trunk. The acute form of parapsoriasis is morphologically different from psoriasis and is usually classified with vasculitis. The plaque form may be a precursor to mycosis fungoides.

DISTRIBUTION PATTERN

a. Psoriasis: extensor surfaces (especially elbows, knees), scalp, trunk, nails, genitalia
b. Lichen planus: buccal mucous membrane, genitalia, flexors (especially wrists, ankles)
c. Pityriasis rosea: bilateral, symmetrical; often involves buccal mucous membranes, palms, and soles
d. Seborrheic dermatitis and inverse psoriasis: scalp, gluteal, umbilical, crural, genital, and flexural areas
e. Secondary syphilis: bilateral, symmetrical; mucous membranes, palms and soles, scalp; no area spared
f. Tinea corporis: asymmetrical; trunk and/or extremities
g. Chronic dermatitis: variable distribution

Chronic Vesiculo-bullous Eruptions

REACTION PATTERNS: By convention, blisters less than 0.5 cm in diameter are referred to as *vesicles*, and those that are larger as *bullae*.

Besides the vesicle of acute dermatitis, there are three morphological types of blisters: (1) the acantholytic vesicle, (2) the tense vesicle (subepidermal), and (3) the viral vesicle.

The acantholytic vesicle or bulla results from the dissolution of the intercellular tonofibrils of the prickle cells, leading to the histological appearance of acantholysis. The loss of cohesion between cells, as a result of this phenomenon, produces vesicles that rupture easily and are, therefore, flaccid from the loss of blister fluid. Gentle pressure on a blister of this type causes the blister to extend laterally with ease (Nikolsky sign). Alternately, the epidermis of the edges of the blister can be stripped off with surprising ease by a gentle sliding motion of the palpating finger. This type of blister occurs consistently in the acantholytic diseases.

When the tissue in the vicinity of the basement membrane undergoes dissolution, the vesicle roof consists of the entire thickness of the epidermis. The clinical appearance is that of a tense vesicle or a subepidermal vesicle histologically. The Nicolsky sign is usually absent in eruptions of this type, although fulminant eruptions may occasionally manifest an extreme fragility of the blisters.

In contrast to secondary toxic eruptions of viral infections, the blisters that result from a direct viral infection of the epidermal cells have a suggestive morphologic pattern of development. The vesicles are usually tense and clear in the early phase, although acantholysis cells of distinctive appearance can be seen microscopically. However, these vesicles quickly become cloudy or turbid and often assume an umbilicated appearance within a few days. This form of blister rarely becomes larger than a centimeter in diameter, even though the eruption may become widely disseminated.

ACANTHOLYTIC DISEASES (intradermal vesicle)
Pemphigus vulgaris is a bullous eruption which usually terminates in death if the condition is not adequately treated. The bulla is fragile and flaccid, often developing on an uninflamed base. Multiple shallow ulcerations are common and very rapidly become tender. The blister can be extended peripherally with ease by gentle pressure, or the epidermis can be stripped off easily by lateral movement of a finger pressing gently on the unaffected skin at the edge of the bullae (Nikolsky sign). Buccal mucous membrane lesions are common.

Pemphigus foliaceus and its variant *pemphigus erythematosus* also are acantholytic diseases. The acantholysis, however, occurs primarily at the level of the stratum granulosum, and the course of the disease is usually not as serious as in pemphigus vulgaris. The Nikolsky sign is demonstrable.

Benign chronic familial pemphigus (Hailey and Hailey) is also an acantholytic disease manifesting the

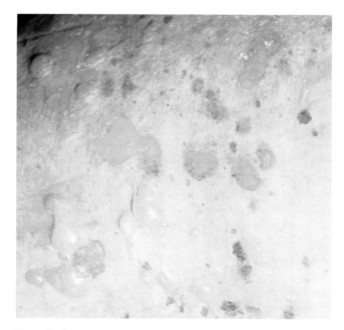

Figure 19. Pemphigus vulgaris

Nikolsky sign. The lesions appear on the friction areas – neck, axilla, and groin – and frequently become secondarily infected with bacteria and yeast. The disease appears to be inherited as a dominant trait.

Keratosis follicularis (Darier disease), although an acantholytic disease, usually does not manifest as a vesicular eruption. The lesions are small, warty, keratotic papules which may coalesce to become foul-smelling, vegetating masses.

Figure 20. Darier disease

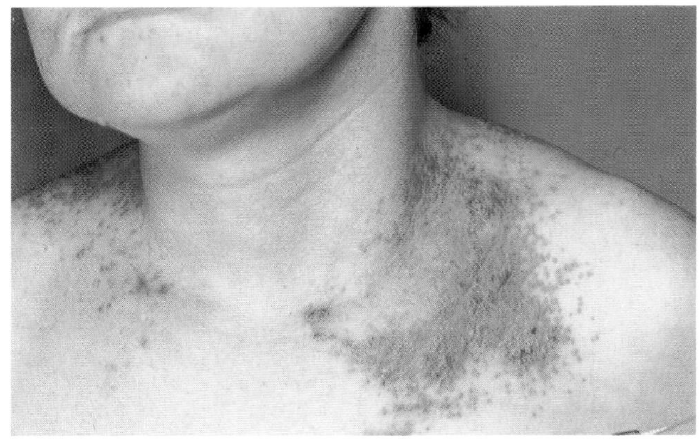

DISEASES WITH SUBEPIDERMAL VESICLES (clinically, tense vesicles)

Dermatitis herpetiformis is a chronic, recurrent, itching eruption with vesicles appearing in clusters. The lesions are usually distributed on the extensor surfaces of the extremities and on the shoulder and pelvic girdle areas of the trunk. The buccal mucous membranes, palms, and soles are usually spared. The eruption is suppressed by oral therapy with sulfapyridine or the sulfones.

Erythema multiforme, as the name implies, may appear as erythematous, purpuric, urticarial, gangrenous, or bullous lesions. The lesions tend to assume ringed or circinate morphology and affect the buccal mucous membrane and the distal parts of the extremities with high frequency. The bilateral, symmetrical distribution indicates inciting agents of internal origin – drugs, infections, and occasionally radiation therapy for other visceral diseases.

Porphyria cutanea tarda frequently appears as a blistering eruption on the face and exposed areas of the extremities, which heals with shallow eschars, cicatrices, and pigmentation. Hirsutism is more noticeable in women. The eruption is a manifestation of a disturbance in porphyrin metabolism and can be confirmed by quantitative porphyrin assays of the urine, stool, and blood.

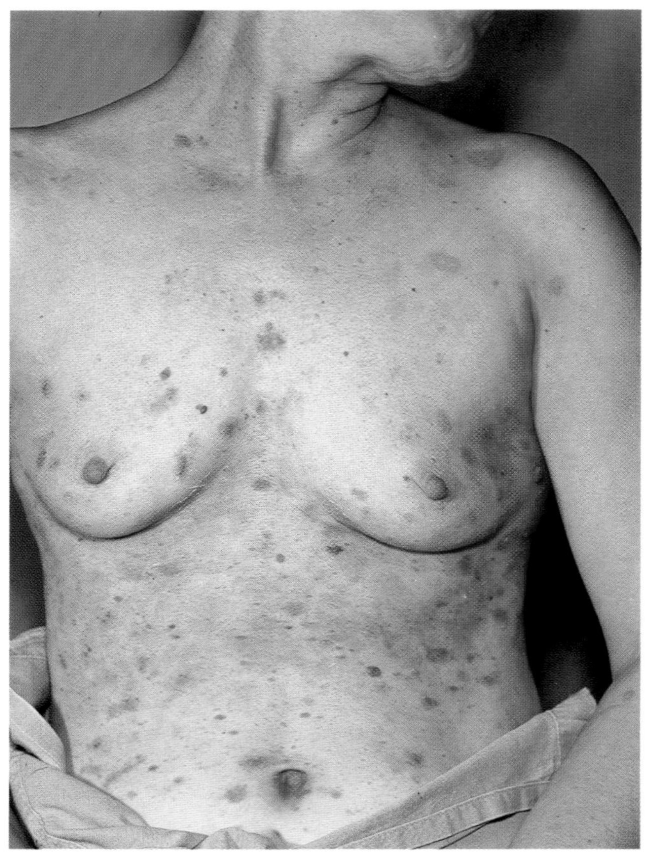

Figure 21. Pemphigus erythematodes

Figure 22. (top) Dermatitis herpetiformis

Figure 23. (middle) Erythema multiforme

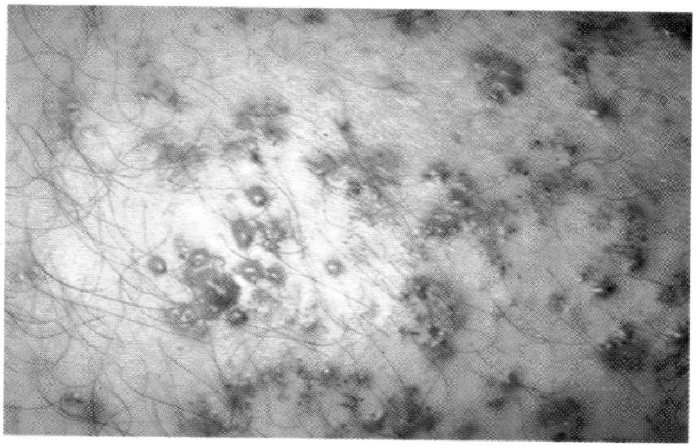

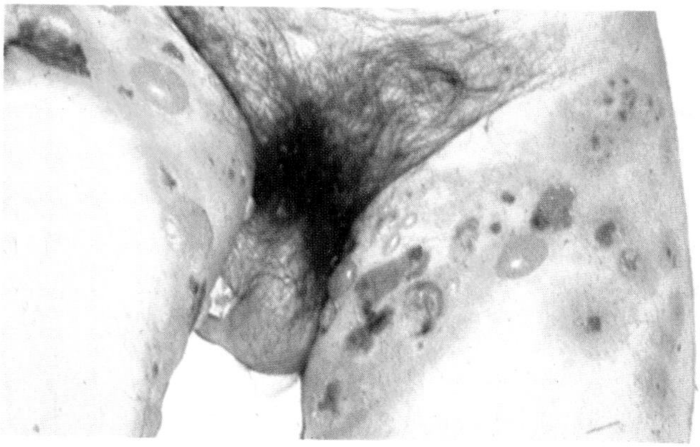

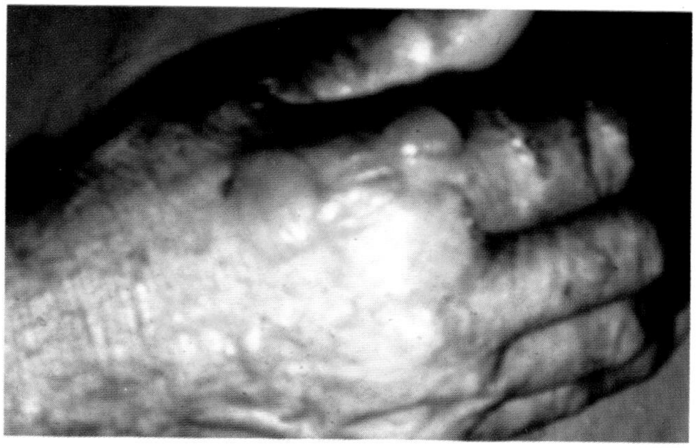

Figure 24. Porphyria cutaneous tarda

Figure 25. (top) Epidermolysis bullosa

Figure 26. (middle) Bullous pemphigoid of the arm

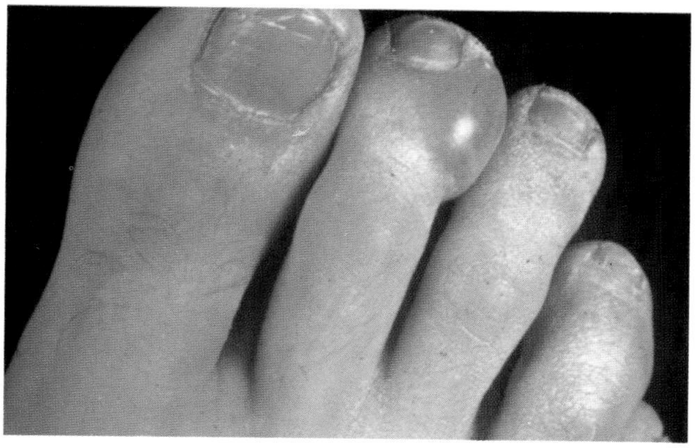

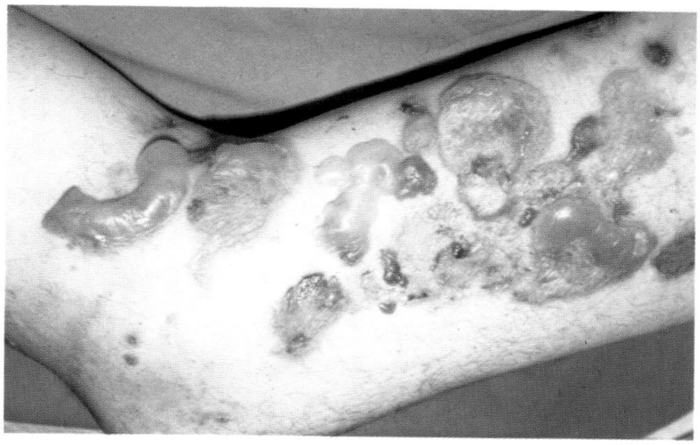

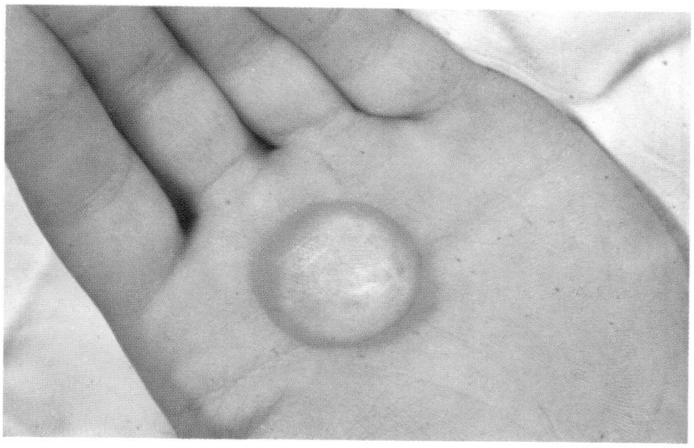

Figure 27. Pressure bulla

Figure 28. Herpes zoster

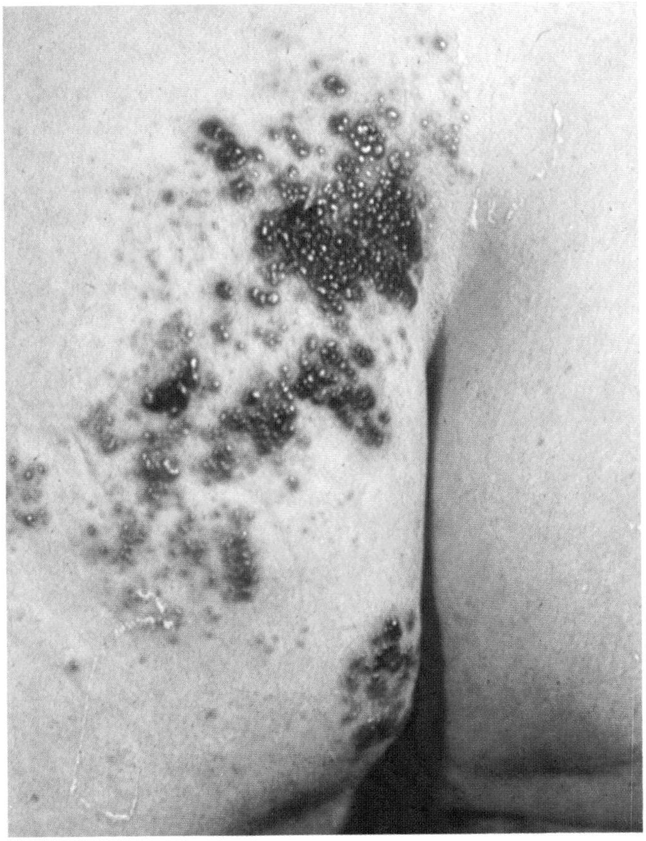

Epidermolysis bullosa is an inherited susceptibility to epidermal separation following trauma. Consequently, the blisters appear on the knuckles, elbows, knees, and feet with high frequency. In the dystrophic forms the eruptions eventually lead to deformity of the extremities. In the simple forms the recurrent blisters are followed frequently by atrophic or hyperplastic scars.

HERPETIC DISEASES
(primary intracellular damage)

Herpes simplex upon initial infection is usually subclinical but may produce an acute gingivostomatitis or vulvovaginitis in children. The herpes simplex eruption may occur as recurrent clusters of vesicles on the lip, orbital tissues, or genitalia. Recurrences may be triggered by exposure to sunlight, emotional stress, menses, and fever. The apparent disappearance of the virus between bouts of vesiculation is thought to be a manifestation of lysogeny. The vesicles, which are initially clear, rapidly become opaque and umbilicated.

The primary infection of *varicella zoster* is well known as a febrile, bilateral, symmetrical "drop of water" vesicular eruption on the extremities and trunk, with a propensity for centripetal distribution. Buccal mucous membrane lesions are common. The lesions rapidly become pustular, umbilicated, and finally crusted. Under various triggering conditions, the blisters may appear in later life in a segmental fashion. The virus usually originates in the dorsal ganglion or its analogues and produces a cutaneous eruption along the nerve endings represented by it. This is thought to be a manifestation of lysogeny. If the latent virus is activated by some nonspecific event, the clinical entity of zoster, with involvement of skin, nerve, and possibly the eye, may appear in conjunction with an early rise in antibody titer within a few days.

A patient with chronic leukemia or lymphoma may have a defective immune mechanism. If zoster occurs, the defective immune mechanism will fail to keep the virus localized, and it may disseminate, producing a viremia with generalized skin and visceral lesions.

OTHER CAUSES OF VESICULOBULLOUS ERUPTIONS

Physical factors:

(a) Heat, x-ray, ultraviolet light or (b) intense cold from solid carbon dioxide or liquid nitrogen.

Chemical agents:

(a) Strong acids, oxidizing agents, and reducing agents or (b) cantharides.

Pyodermas

Primary Bacterial Infections

Infection of the skin by bacteria is usually the result of (a) altered resistance of the host (antibiotics, corticosteroids, intercurrent disease), (b) injury to the skin giving a portal of entry, or (c) overwhelming inoculation. REACTION PATTERNS: Erythema, pustule, abscess.

STAPHYLOCOCCAL PYODERMAS

Although staphylococcus aureus is a part of the resident flora of childhood, it is usually not a part of the adult flora. Nevertheless, 20% of adults are persistent nasal carriers of staphylococci and another 60% are intermittent carriers. From the nasal area, organisms move out to the skin where they may produce disease.

It has been estimated that 5% to 9% of the population each year have cutaneous staphylococcal infection severe enough to warrant medical attention. In general, staphylococcal infections may involve either the skin surface or the hair follicles.

Impetigo is the most-common skin infection caused by a staphylococcal pathogen, although, less frequently, beta-hemolytic streptococci may also be the causative agent. Frequently, there is a mixture of both organisms.

The disease usually occurs in children and has a higher incidence when poor health and nutrition and inadequate personal hygiene are prevalent. The lesion begins as a small thin-walled vesicle which soon ruptures, leaving a weeping denuded spot. This rapidly forms a thick, yellowish crust which appears to be stuck on the skin. The process may extend beneath the crusts, and satellite vesicles and pustules are common. Although the disease is usually confined to the face, other areas may be involved. In impetigo the process is quite superficial and involves only the upper layers of the epidermis. When not properly treated, the process may become quite extensive and, if primarily of streptococcal origin, may lead to glomerulonephritis.

In *ecthyma*, the process is deeper and erodes through the epidermis into the upper dermis. The disease usually occurs on the legs of children and is characterized by small pustules arising from erythematous bases. These erode and form crusts which cover the underlying erosion. In contrast to impetigo, scarring is common because of the depth of the process.

Figure 29. Impetigo

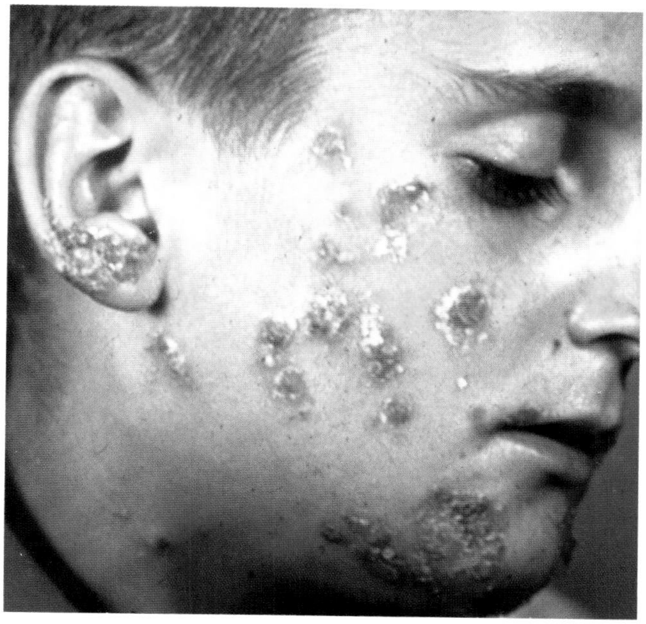

The hair follicle serves as a common portal of entry for staphylococcal infection. In the most superficial form of follicular-initiated infection, *folliculitis*, the process is confined to the external portion of the individual follicles. The clinical lesion is a follicular papule or pustule, and the inflammatory reaction is limited.

When the infection occurs deeper in the follicle, a variety of clinical pictures may result. Folliculitis of the bearded area is known as *sycosis vulgaris* and may be chronic. Men with moustaches and beards are more susceptible to this infection. A similar process involving the cilia of the eyelids results in a *hordeolum* (sty) or inflammation of the sebaceous glands of the eye.

The *furuncle* (boil) represents a deep follicular infec-

Figure 30. (top) Bullous impetigo on the forearms
Figure 31. (middle) Ecthyma, calf

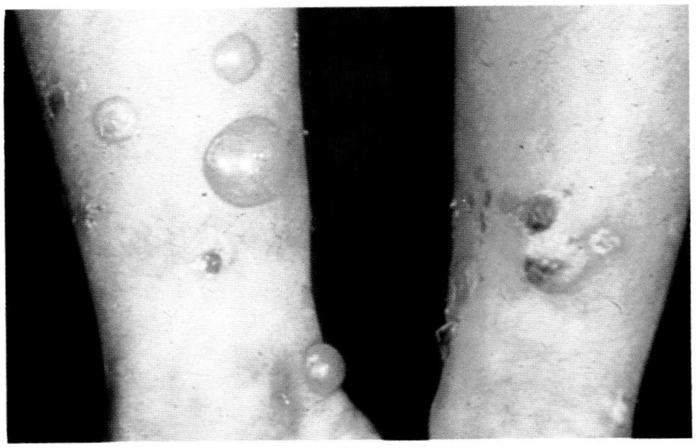

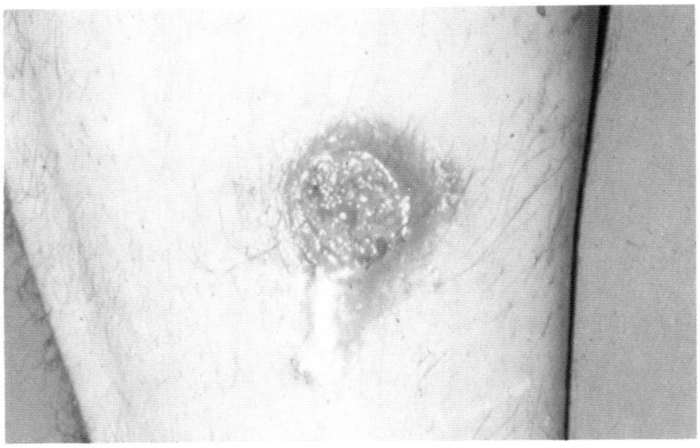

tion with a marked inflammatory reaction. The clinical lesion is an erythematous nodule surrounding a hair follicle. As the lesion progresses, the nodule becomes fluctuant, the apex thins, and the lesion ruptures to expel pus and a necrotic core.

Still deeper involvement results in the *carbuncle*, a lesion encompassing several adjacent hair follicles. This lesion presents as a large erythematous mass which drains to the skin surface through several openings.

The more superficial and localized staphylococcal pyodermas can be treated locally with judicious cleansing of the involved areas, removal of all crusts, and application of an antibiotic ointment. Deeper and more-extensive infection will require therapy with an appropriate systemic antibiotic.

STREPTOCOCCAL PYODERMAS

Beta-hemolytic streptococci are not a part of the normal cutaneous flora, although nonpathogenic streptococci are found on the skin of children and elderly people. Beta-hemolytic streptococci colonize in the pharynx and may be transient on the skin in approximately 0.5% to 1% of the population as a result of contamination from the nose and throat.

Streptococcal skin infection is of considerable clini-

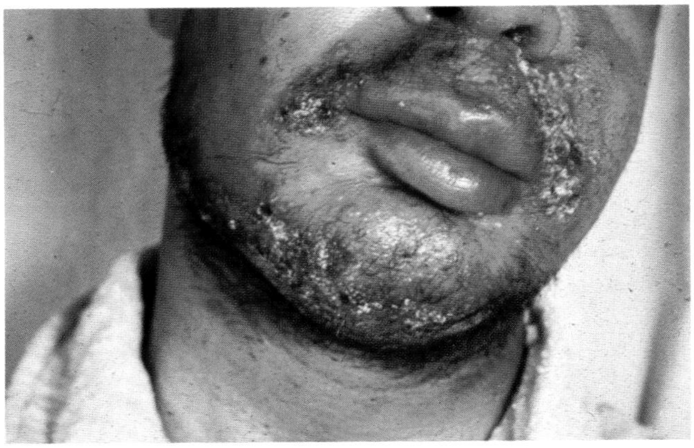

Figure 32. Sycosis vulgaris

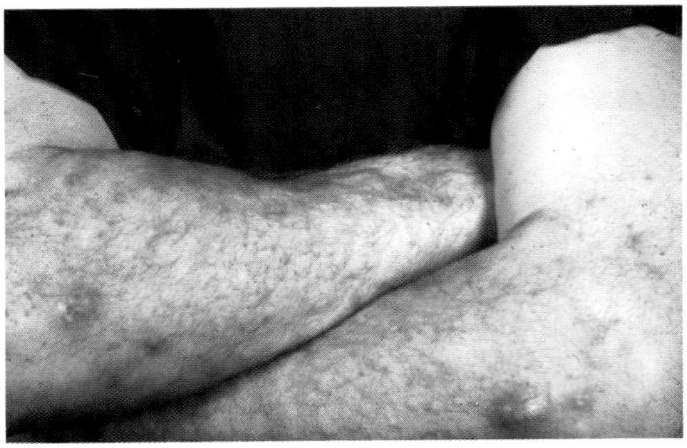

Figure 33. Furuncles on forearms

Figure 34. Erysipelas

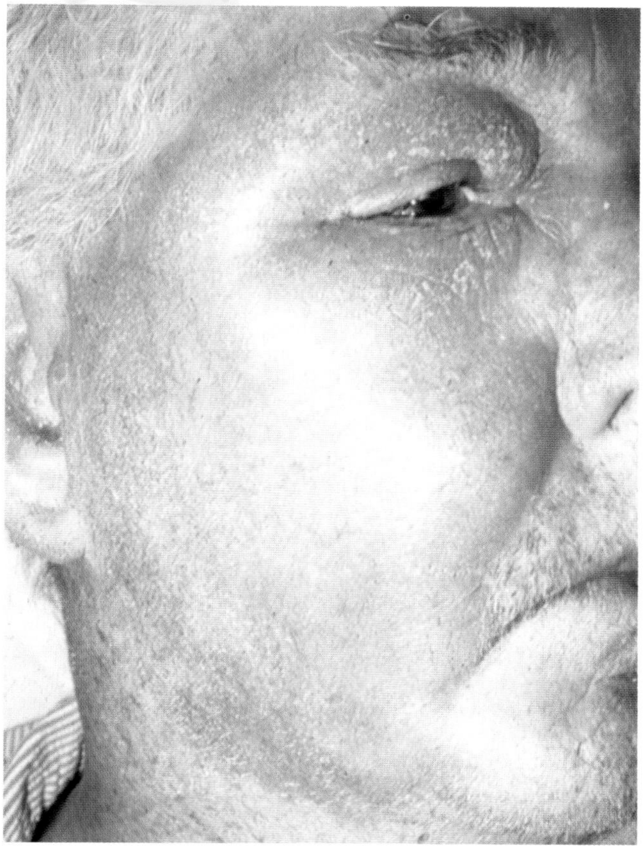

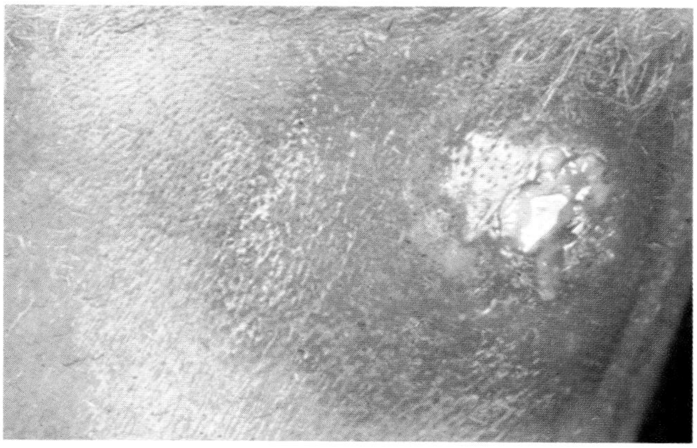

Figure 35. Carbuncle on neck

cal importance, as it can be complicated by glomerulonephritis. In certain tropical and subtropical areas, streptococcal pyoderma is a more-common antecedent of glomerulonephritis than is streptococcal pharyngitis.

The basic pattern of staphylococcal infection is circumscription of the individual lesions, whereas skin invasion by streptococci produces a spreading cellulitis and early lymphatic involvement.

A characteristic form of superficial streptococcal cellulitis is *erysipelas*. This disease usually occurs on the face, scalp, or lower extremities and is frequently heralded by a severe systemic reaction, including headache, high fever, and malaise. The skin lesion begins as a small, sharply defined patch of erythema which rapidly spreads peripherally. The involved skin is warm and edematous and the border is easily palpable.

Other forms of streptococcal cellulitis are less distinctive and usually consist of a spreading, brawny edema of the skin and subcutaneous tissue accompanied by erythema and tenderness.

Beta-hemolytic streptococci may be the etiologic agent responsible for impetigo and ecthyma, although a staphylococcal origin is much more common.

Besides primary streptococcal skin disease, this organism can also produce secondary infection in preexisting dermatoses such as intertrigo and the various eczematous dermatitides.

Because of the possibility of nephritis, systemic antibiotics play an important role in the therapy of streptococcal skin disease. Local measures such as warm compresses and rest are also important.

Secondary Bacterial Infections

Secondary invasion of the skin by pathogenic bacteria occurs when there is damage to the skin; e.g., dermatitis, ulcerations, and intertrigo. Specific infections are seen in amebiasis cutis, tularemia, leishmaniasis. An infection may also occur as a cutaneous infection of a systemic disease; for example, pyoderma gangrenosum has been regarded as a manifestation of ulcerative colitis.

Figure 36. (top) Pyoderma gangrenosum of leg

Figure 37. (bottom) Amebiasis cutis on the arms

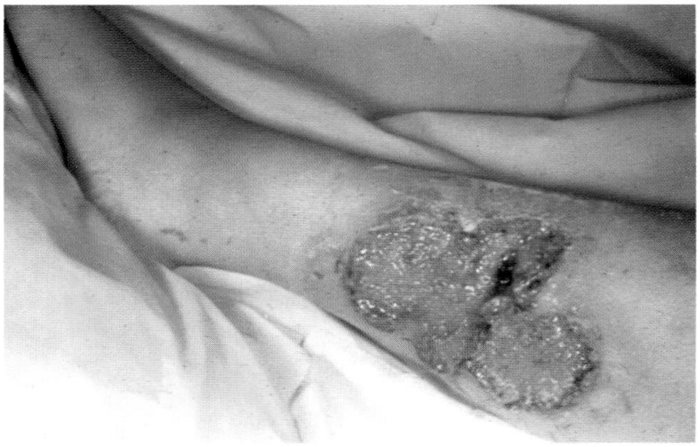

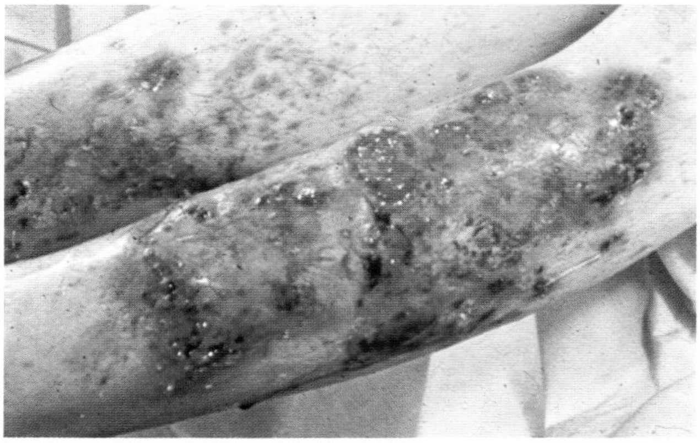

Dermatophytosis
(Fungal Infections)

Figure 38. Tinea capitis due to M. audouini

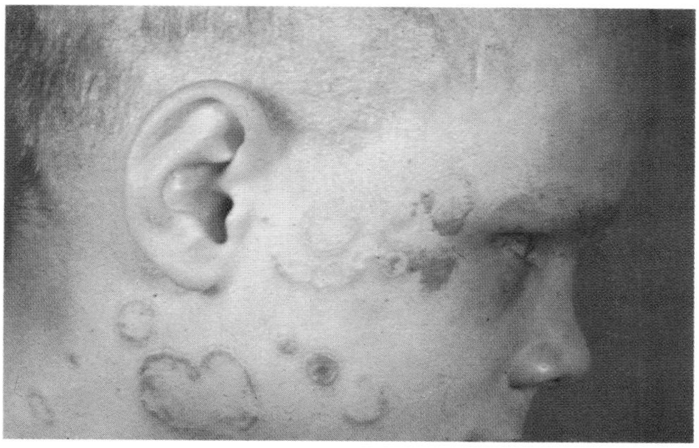

Dermatophytes are defined as fungi that produce superficial cutaneous infection (dermatophytosis) involving the skin, hair, and nails. They do not invade living tissue as do the bacteria.

The dermatophytes are included in three genera: *Microsporum*, which usually attacks hair; *Trichophyton*, which attacks skin, hair, and nails; and *Epidermophyton*, which usually attacks skin. Thus, dermatophytes may show considerable specificity for the type of keratin that they invade.

TINEA CAPITIS

The disease begins with a round to oval patch that shows dull, gray, broken hairs and partial alopecia. The original patch slowly enlarges and is usually followed by new patches; eventually the entire scalp may be involved. The process reaches its fullest extent after several months and may remain in a chronic state for several years without treatment.

Although tinea capitis caused by *M. audouini* is usually noninflammatory, infection with other organisms such as *M. canis* may produce a markedly inflammatory condition known as kerion. Such inflammatory processes are usually self-limited and resolve spontaneously.

TINEA CORPORIS: TINEA CIRCINATA

The most characteristic form presents a small erythematous papule which gradually enlarges peripherally to form a ringed (annular) lesion. The center of the lesion frequently clears as it enlarges. The border of the lesion is usually raised, erythematous, and occasionally vesicular. Some scaling is common. In tinea corporis the process is seldom widespread, and the lesions are usually limited to one or two.

TINEA CRURIS

Tinea cruris, or ringworm of the groin, is very common in males although rare in females. *E. floccosum*, *T. men-*

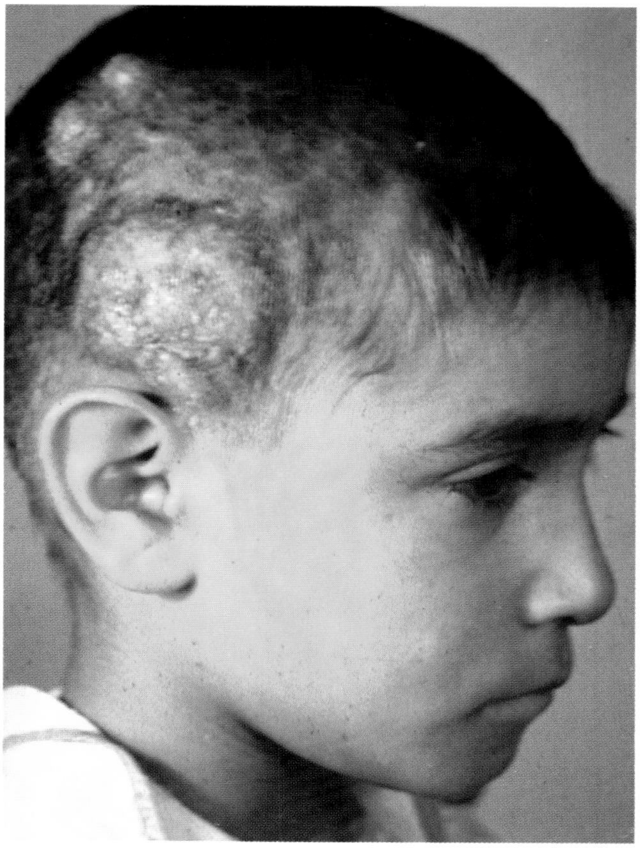

Figure 39. Tinea capitis due to M. canis

Figure 40. Tinea circinata

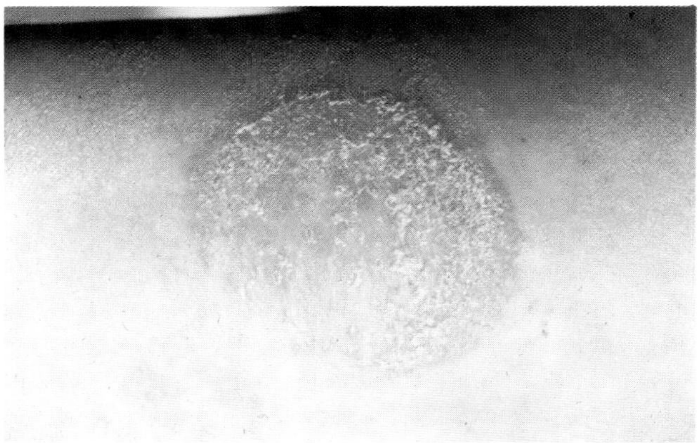

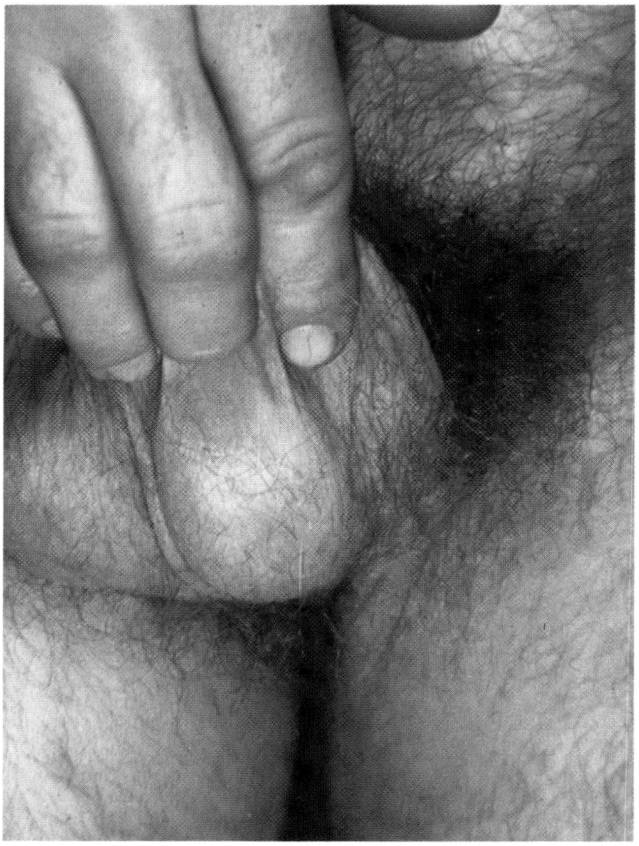

Figure 41. Tinea cruris

tagrophytes, and *T. rubrum* are the causative organisms in most cases. The infection symmetrically involves the upper inner thighs and extends outward from the crural fold in large circinate lesions. The lesions range in color from dull reddish-brown to bright red, with the borders usually elevated and occasionally vesicular.

TINEA PEDIS

Of all dermatophyte infections, tinea pedis is the most common. The disease is widespread in the adult male population, although relatively uncommon in women and children. Not all eruptions of the feet are caused by fungi. This simple fact is frequently overlooked, resulting in inappropriate antifungal therapy for a diversity of foot eruptions including contact dermatitis, simple intertrigo, psoriasis, and pyoderma.

Intertriginous tinea pedis is the most common form and begins in the toe webs, especially in the fourth interspace which is subject to the greatest heat, moisture,

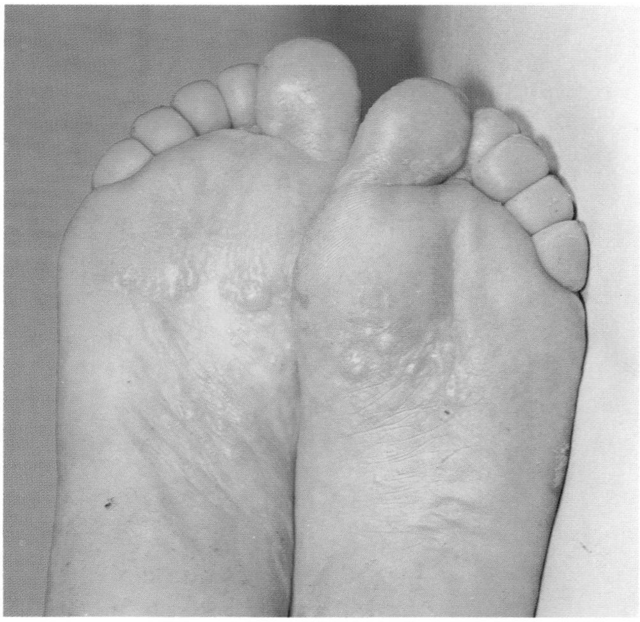

Figure 42. Tinea pedis

Figure 43. (top) Tinea pedis
Figure 44. (middle) Dermatophytid of palms and fingers

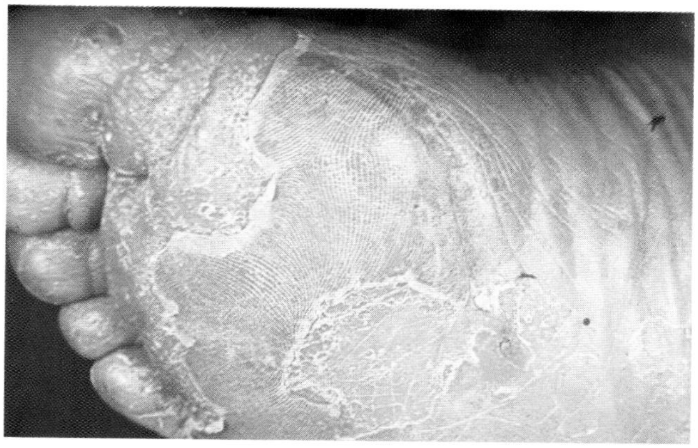

and opportunity for maceration. Clinically, moist scaling, fissuring, maceration, and variable degrees of erythema are observed between the toes. The patient may be asymptomatic but often complains of itching or burning. Intertriginous tinea pedis commonly extends to the under surfaces of the toes and occasionally to the anterior plantar surface. Fungal involvement of the dorsum of the toes and feet is uncommon.

The usual organism responsible for this fungus infection is *T. mentagrophytes*, although *T. rubrum* may produce a chronic type of infection, or *E. floccosum* may occasionally be involved in maceration of the toe webs.

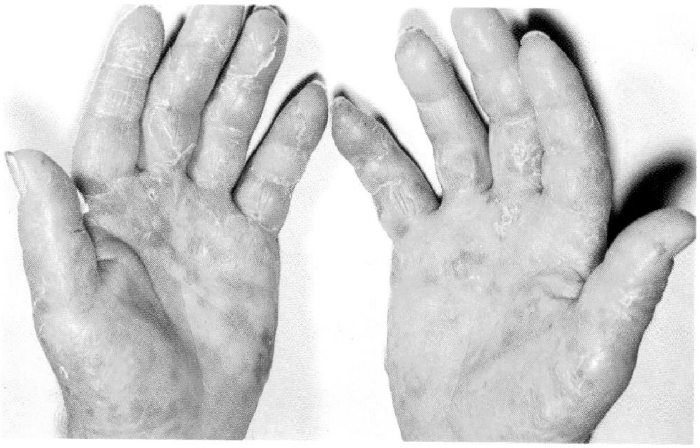

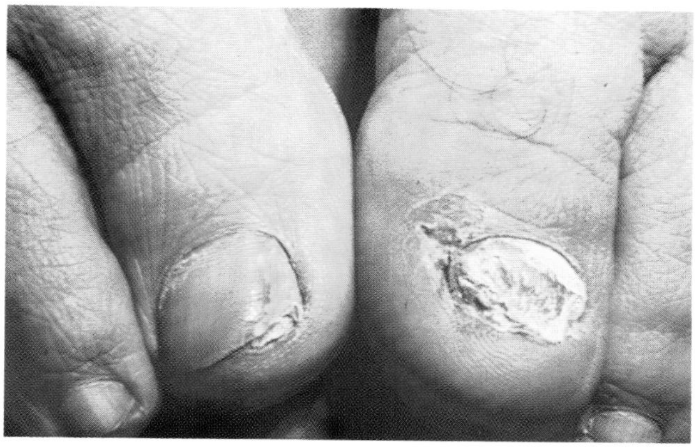

Figure 45. Onchomycoses

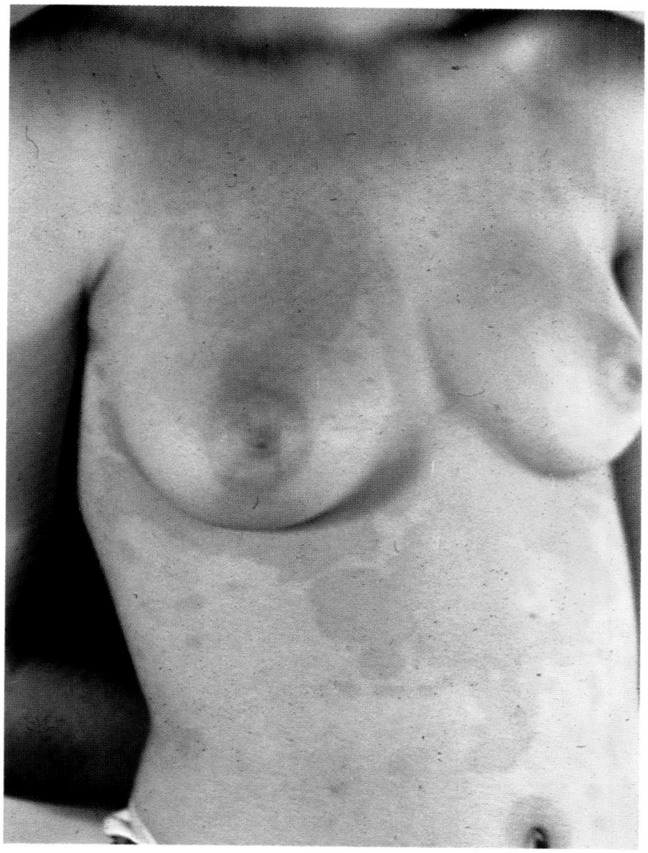

Figure 46. Tinea versicolor

Dermatophyte infection of the nails, *tinea unguium* (onychomycosis), involves the toenails more frequently than the fingernails and begins with localized areas of discoloration beneath the nail. The nail plate becomes lusterless and gradually thickens. Ultimately, the nail may become greatly distorted with marked thickening, cracking, and piling up of loose keratinous debris.

Dermatophytid refers to an allergic reaction or secondary eruption, usually on the fingers and hands, due to an active dermatophyte infection that occurs at an area removed from the actual infection. Thus, dermatophytids of the palms are not uncommon with active tinea pedis. In these cases the "id" reaction usually presents as a vesicular eruption from which fungi cannot be demonstrated. In all types of dermatophyte reactions, the patient will show a delayed hypersensitivity to the common dermatophyte antigen trichophytin.

TINEA VERSICOLOR

This superficial dermatomycosis is caused by the fungus Malassezia furfur. When exposed to sunlight, the uninfected skin will tan but the infected skin will peel and appear to be partially depigmented.

Candidiasis (Moniliasis)

Candidiasis is a fungus infection that usually is superficially confined to the skin and mucous membranes but is occasionally capable of causing lesions in viscera, which are serious to life. It is usually attributable to one species of fungus, *Candida albicans*.

Etiology

a. Incidence of infection increases with age of patient.
b. Organism is a common inhabitant of the gastrointestinal tract as a saprophyte.
c. Debilitating or systemic illness, diabetes, and obesity decrease resistance to the organism.
d. Moisture, in the form of hyperhidrosis, or prolonged immersion in water favors propagation of the organism.
e. Organism probably changes from saprophytic to pathogenic type under certain circumstances.
f. Overuse of antibiotics is prone to increase growth of pathogenic candidiasis.

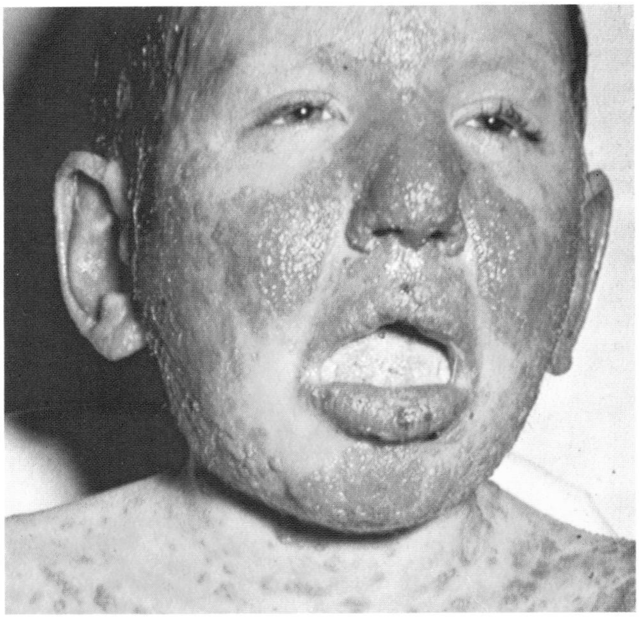

Figure 47. Monilial granuloma

Miscellaneous Diseases

ONYCHIA AND PARONYCHIA

These ailments have been blamed on both moniliasis and bacterial infection, but the real cause is probably mechanical.

a. Seen most often in cooks, salad makers, fruit peelers, and dishwashers.
b. Paronychial tissues first involved.
c. Nail has transverse ridges with no loss of shine.
d. Nail is thickened and distorted.
e. Onycholysis, separation of the nail from its underlying bed, may occur.

INTERTRIGINOUS DERMATITIS

Common sites are axillae, groin, umbilicus, intergluteal and inframammary folds, and interdigital webs of the feet.

a. Lesions are present as bright-red, exuding patches with scalloped borders.
b. The usual cause is obesity combined with the lack of aeration and the evaporation of sweat.
c. Small, flaccid vesiculopustules often appear outside of zone of intertrigo.

EROSIO INTERDIGITALIS BLASTOMYCETIA

Intertrigo affects the outer digital web of hands – bright-red base with peeling border. Because of the difficulty in separating the ring finger from the middle finger, this finger web is often involved and given the above descriptive term.

PERLÈCHE

a. Inflammation and erosion at angles of the mouth.
b. Bright-red base; surface has pellicle with frequent fissures.
c. Fungus infection, usually *Candida;* Vitamin B deficiency, weight loss, advancing age, and streptococci

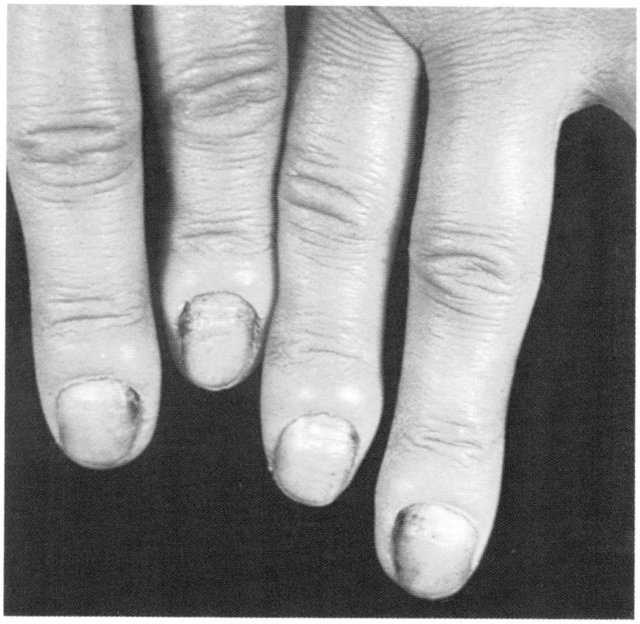

Figure 48. Paronychia

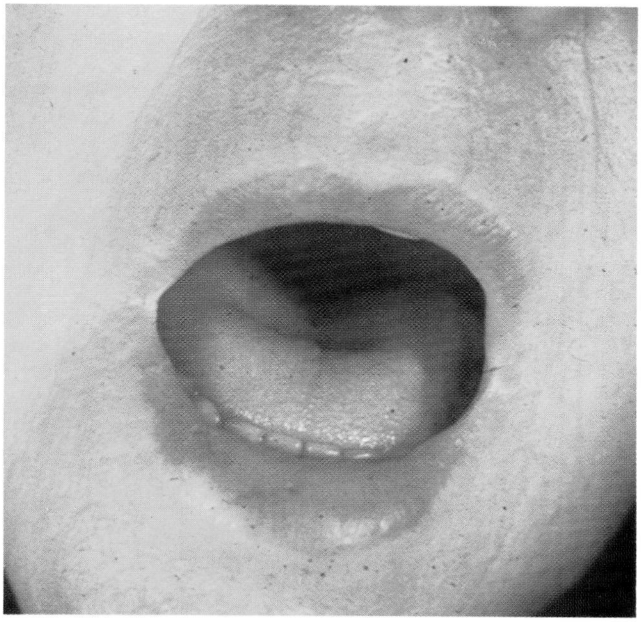

Figure 49. Perlèche

Figure 50. Thrush moniliasis

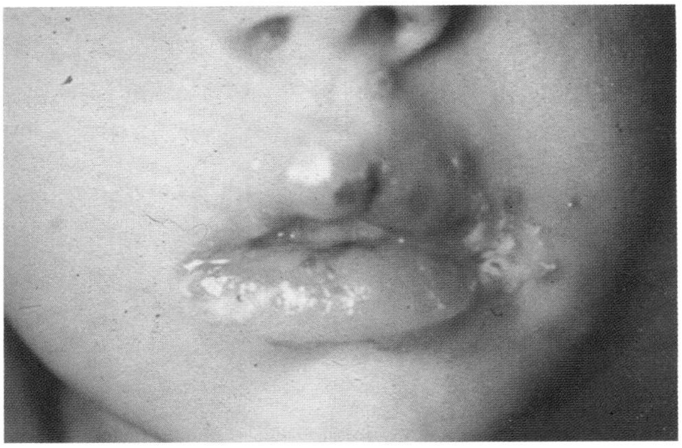

have all been found to be causative factors.

d. Frequently, a mechanical cause is the primary agent, and often new, well-fitted dentures are most helpful.

ORAL CANDIDIASIS (thrush)

Monilial granuloma

a. Seen most commonly in infants, aged, diabetics, and during long-time treatment with corticosteroids or orally administered antibiotics.
b. Often begins in early childhood as oral thrush and later tends to settle on the hands, feet, face, and scalp.
c. Whitish, loosely adherent membrane is attached to oral mucosa or forms lesions with large incrustations which can break off, leaving bleeding granulomatous bases.

SUPERFICIAL GLOSSITIS

A beefy-red, smooth, sometimes mottled tongue is associated with stomatitis, which can be the result of a myriad of factors of which the etiology remains completely obscure.

PRURITUS ANI

Severe itching with maceration around the anus or genitals, resulting from a variety of factors. It appears to be a symptom complex and can develop into a chronic condition if not treated properly.

Pigmentation Disorders

The color of the normal skin is determined by several different pigments including melanin, oxyhemoglobin, reduced hemoglobin, and carotene. In certain diseases, endogenous pigments such as bilirubin may be important, while in other diseases exogenous pigments such as heavy metals may play a role.

MELANIN PIGMENTATION

The most common pigmentary change associated with systemic disease is disordered melanin pigmentation. Melanin is an insoluble brown or black pigment produced by enzymatic oxidation of the substrate tyrosine. The end product is bound to protein and exists in a highly polymerized state.

Melanin synthesis occurs in the melanocyte, a mature cell residing in the basal layer of the epidermis. The progenator of the melanocyte, the melanoblast, is presumed to migrate from its neural crest site to its final epidermal resting place during embryonic development.

During melanin synthesis, the copper-containing enzyme tyrosinase reacts with the substrate tyrosine during which a distinctive granule, the melanosome, is formed within the cytoplasm of the melanocytes. Through a series of oxidative reactions, these melanosomes are transformed into the end product, melanin granules. Within the basal layer of the epidermis, the melanocytes lie in close apposition to the basal cells, and through a process known as cytocrine transfer, melanin granules are passed through dendritic processes of the melanocytes into adjacent epidermal cells where they provide the melanin pigmentation normally seen in the skin.

Besides its synthesis in the epidermis, melanin is also formed in the mucous membranes, hair bulb, uveal tract, retinal pigment epithelium, and leptomeninges.

EXTERNAL (PHYSICAL) CAUSES OF HYPERPIGMENTATION

1. Ultraviolet light
2. Photosensitive substances, internally or externally, in the presence of sunlight
3. Alpha rays of thorium X
4. Roentgen rays
5. Heat
6. Severe erythema–pigmentation (heat, caustics, mechanical irritation, pruritus)
7. Dermatological diseases such as
   a. Dermatitis herpetiformis
   b. Vagabond disease (pediculosis corporis)
   c. Postinflammatory melanosis
   Mongolian spots, pigmented nevi, malignant neoplasms, blue nevi, seborrheic keratosis, malignant melanomas, lichen planus.

Etiology and Types of Pigmentation

NUTRITIONAL CAUSES

Deficiencies of several vitamins and nutritional factors can produce pigmentary changes. Starvation may produce pigmentation of the face (melasma) followed by more-generalized pigmentation. In vitamin A deficiency, follicular hyperkeratosis with hyperpigmentation in a follicular pattern is frequently observed. The bulbar conjunctiva may also undergo pigmentation. It is suggested that hyperpigmentation may be due to a reduced concentration of the normal inhibitors of melanin synthesis.

Pellagra resulting from a diet deficient in nicotinic acid presents the classic triad of dermatitis, diarrhea, and dementia. The dermatitis usually has an acute eczematous phase and is generally localized to the exposed areas such as the face, neck, "V" area of the chest (Casal necklace), and the forearms and hands. Pigmentation typically occurs as the acute phase of the dermatitis subsides and is a tan to bronze color. Roughened hyperkeratotic pigmented areas over pressure points such as the elbows and knees are characteristic of pellagra.

HORMONAL CAUSES

Pituitary-Adrenal Axis: A number of diseases of the pituitary-adrenal axis can result in hyperpigmentation. The normal pituitary elaborates melanocyte-stimulating hormone (MSH), a compound closely related in structure to adrenocorticotropic hormone (ACTH). This hormone controls the activity of the pigment-producing melanocytes, and changes in its output by the pituitary are reflected in changes in pigmentation. The level of MSH production is determined primarily by the level of circulating corticoids, and thus the pattern of MSH elaboration is similar to that of ACTH.

Clinical conditions and physiologic states associated with increased activity of the pituitary gland, such as pregnancy, Addison disease, and acromegaly frequently exhibit an increase in melanin pigmentation. Decreased pituitary function, as in panhypopituitarism, is associated with a relative decrease in melanin pigmentation.

Hyperthyroidism: Hyperpigmentation occurs occasionally in hyperthyroidism. This may be diffuse and widespread or localized to sun-exposed areas. Only rarely is it found in the oral mucous membranes. In pronounced cases, the pigmentation in hyperthyroidism may closely simulate that of Addison disease. Paradoxically, patients with hyperthyroidism have a higher incidence of vitiligo than would be expected.

Sex Hormones: Several altered patterns of sex hormones may be associated with pigmentation. The most

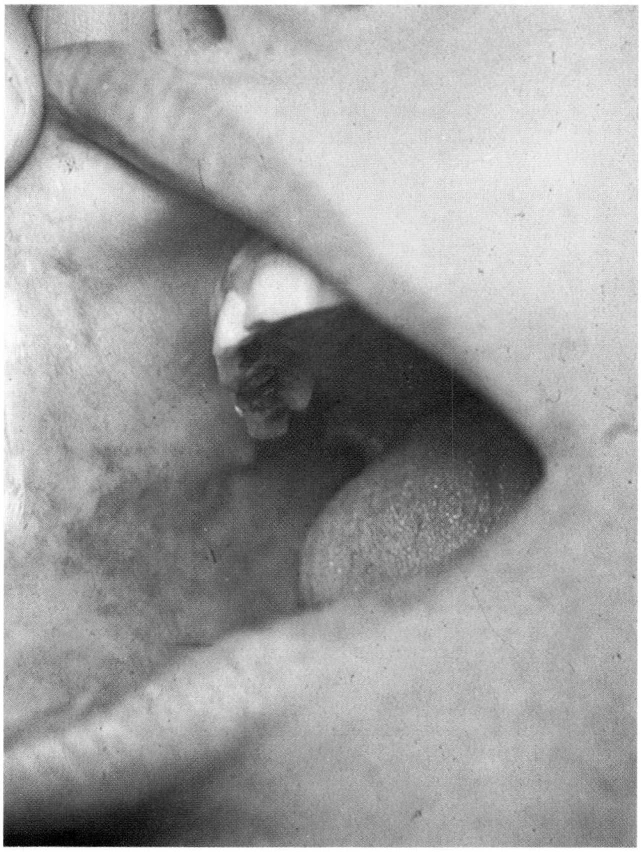

Figure 51. Addison disease, mouth

common of these is pregnancy, in which hyperpigmentation almost always occurs. Symmetrical pigmentation over the face (chloasma gravidarum or mask of pregnancy) and hyperpigmentation of the nipples and areolae are characteristic. The administration of oral contraceptives, with their simulation of the hormone state of pregnancy, frequently produce similar pigmentary changes. The facial pigmentation produced by these drugs may be conspicuous and permanent.

HEMATOPOIETIC AND LYMPHOID DISEASES

In pernicious anemia, the combination of the anemia and a mild bilirubinemia produces the lemon-yellow color characteristic of this disease. There is also a tendency for diffuse or blotchy melanin pigmentation, vitiligo, and premature graying of the hair. In congenital hemolytic anemia and sickle cell anemia, one sees pigmentation of the legs and, frequently, associated ulcerations. The pigmentation is probably a post-inflammatory reaction.

In malignant lymphoma, one may also encounter pigmentation. This is usually diffuse and ranges from bronze to brown in color.

COLLAGEN DISEASES

Although pigmentary changes may be present in lupus erythematosus and dermatomyositis, they are more commonly associated with scleroderma. In this disease, pigmentation varies from a dirty ivory to a deep bronze color and is usually found on the face, hands, arms, and legs. The pathogenesis of this pigmentation is not clear.

GASTROINTESTINAL DISORDERS

Pigmentary abnormalities are encountered in a wide variety of gastrointestinal diseases. In hepatic cirrhosis, there may be diffuse pigmentation, most pronounced on exposed areas. Impaired detoxification of estrogens has been implicated in this situation as it has been in the formation of spider angiomas among cirrhotics.

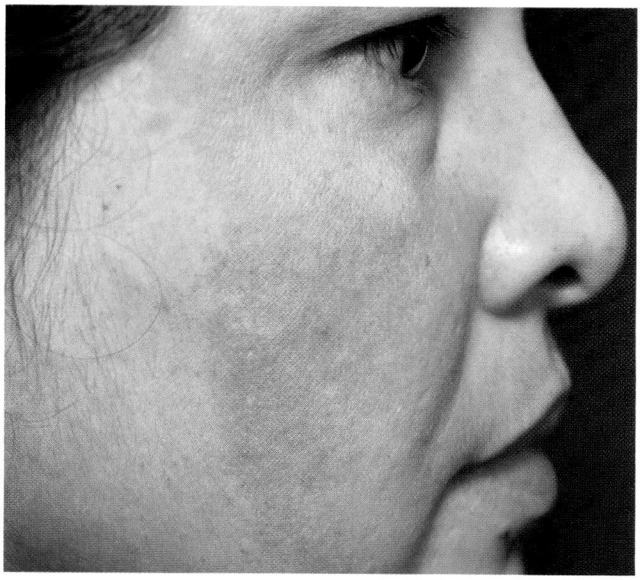

Figure 52. Chloasma

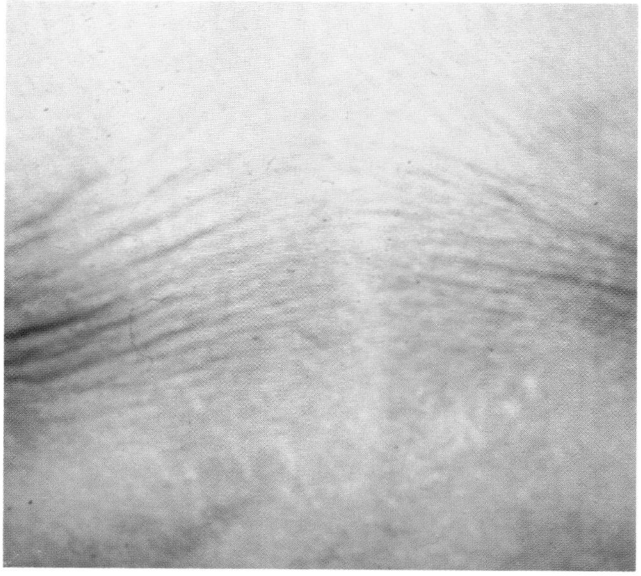

Figure 53. Pigmentation associated with Hodgkin disease

Figure 54. Pigmentation associated with generalized morphea

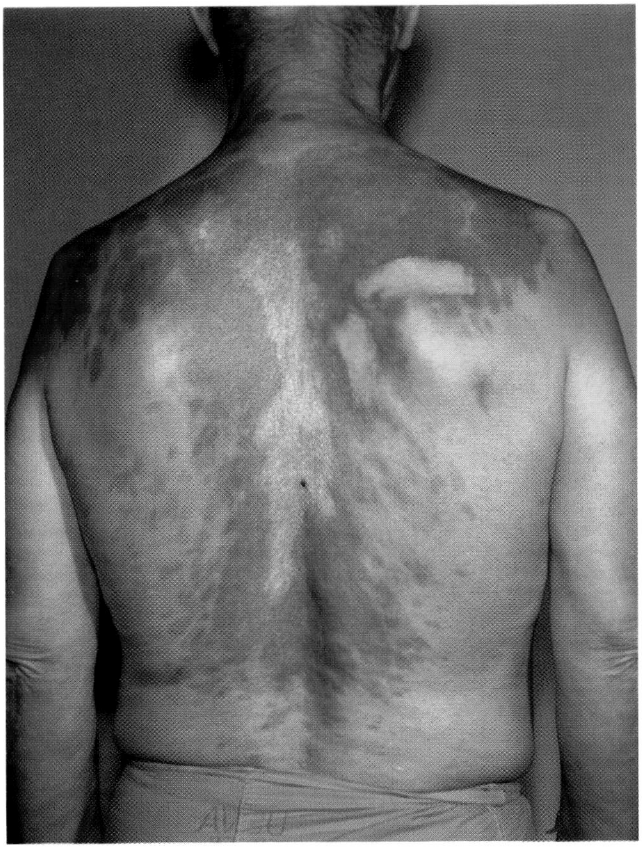

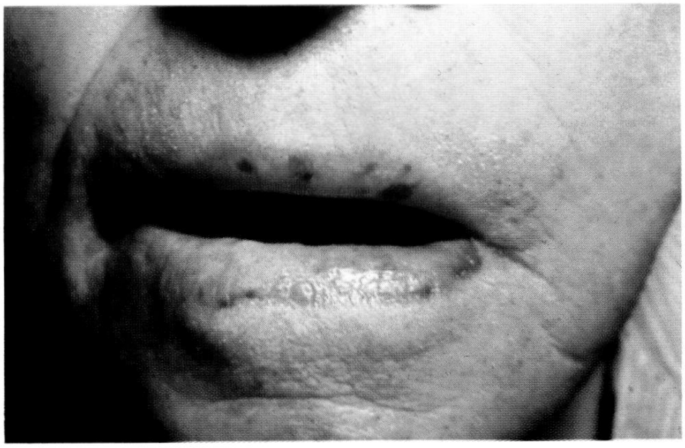

Figure 55. Peutz-Jeghers syndrome

Patients with sprue may develop perioral pigmentation or pigmented patches over wide areas of the body, especially the face. In some cases the pigmentation may resemble Addison disease, but hyperpigmentation to some degree occurs in almost all sprue patients.

The Peutz-Jeghers syndrome is a hereditary abnormality characterized by pigmented macules on the oral mucosa and skin, and polyps of the small intestine. The pigmented lesions are distributed on the lips and oral mucosa and, less frequently, on the fingers and toes. They have the appearance of freckles but are found in different areas than ordinary freckles. The lesions of the small intestine are actually hamartomas and are not related to polyposis of the colon. Although an occasional lesion may undergo malignant transformation, such a change is unusual.

METABOLIC DISEASES

Gaucher disease: This hereditary disorder is characterized by splenomegaly, scleral pingueculae, and skin pigmentation.

Niemann-Pick disease: This is a heredofamilial disease with distinct brownish-yellow discoloration of the skin.

Phenylalanine and Tyrosine: The normal formation of melanin depends upon the enzymatic oxidation of the amino acid tyrosine, and normal amounts of this tyrosine substrate are made available through oxidation of dietary phenylalanine to tyrosine in the liver. In *phenylketonuria,* this conversion of phenylalanine to tyrosine is blocked by lack of activity of the responsible enzyme, phenylalanine hydroxylase.

Besides the mental deficiency that is characteristic of phenylketonuria, these patients show the results of decreased melanin synthesis and characteristically have blue eyes, light hair, and fair complexions.

Alkaptonuria: With this condition, absence of the enzyme homogentisic acid oxidase leads to an accumulation of homogentisic acid, a normal oxidation production of tyrosine. Oxidation of homogentisic acid forms a melanin-like compound which, in a polymerized form, is deposited in cartilagenous tissue to produce a bluish-black pigmentation, ochronosis.

HEMOCHROMATOSIS

In hemochromatosis, a markedly increased absorption of iron leads to its deposition in various organs, including the skin, and produces the clinical picture of generalized hyperpigmentation, diabetes mellitus, cirrhosis of the liver, and cardiac failure. The cutaneous abnormality consists of a diffuse bronze pigmentation.

Although large amounts of iron pigment (hemosiderin) are deposited in the skin in hemochromatosis, the clinical pigmentation is produced primarily by melanin.

NEUROLOGIC DISORDERS

Generalized hyperpigmentation resembling that of Addison disease may occur in a number of central nervous system disorders, presumably from disordered production of MSH. These diseases include schizophrenia, encephalitis, ependymoma, Wilson disease, and Schilder disease.

One of the characteristic features of generalized *neurofibromatosis* (von Recklinghausen disease) is the presence of pigmented patches commonly called café au lait spots.

PHOTOSENSITIVITY

Photosensitization frequently results in residual melanin pigmentation. It is difficult to say in many cases whether stimulation of melanin production is a postinflammatory phenomenon or is effected by ultraviolet rays themselves.

DRUGS

A variety of drugs are capable of producing cutaneous

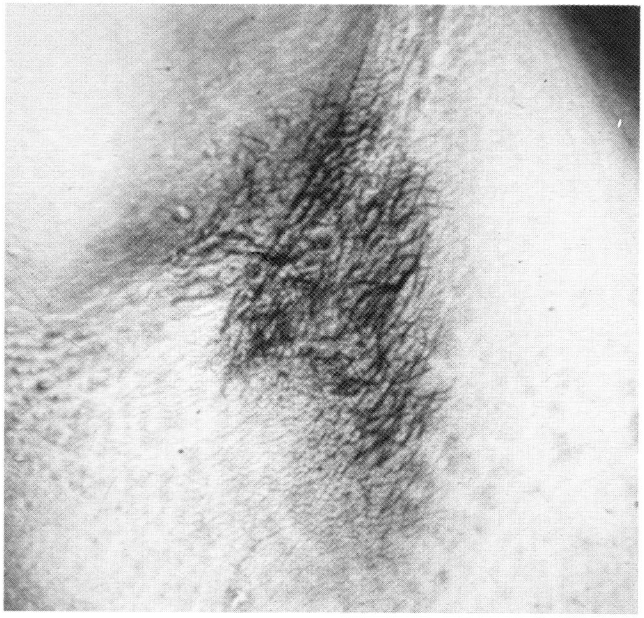

Figure 56. Acanthosis nigricans in the axilla

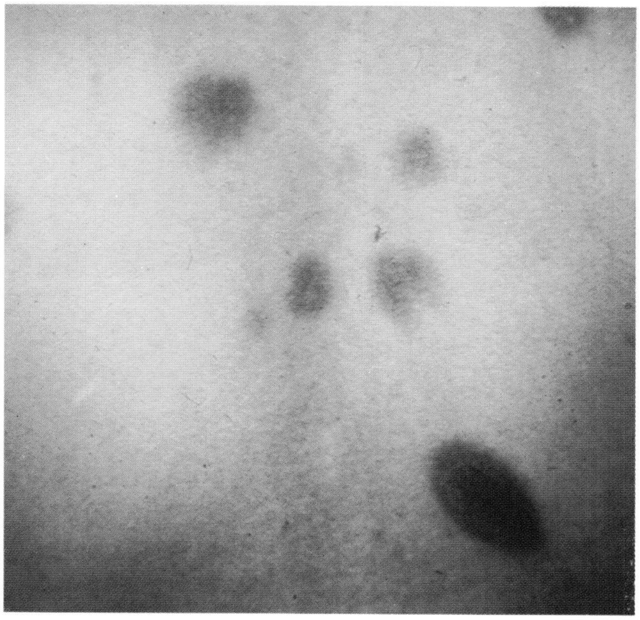

Figure 57. Phenolphthalein eruption

pigmentation. Mesantoin and busulfan have produced widespread diffuse pigmentation; arsenicals also produce extensive pigmentation. In arsenical pigmentation, however, there is a spotty appearance associated with palmar and plantar keratoses.

Various exogenous heavy metals also produce pigmentation. Argyria may result from both industrial and therapeutic uses of silver. The metal is deposited directly in the dermis and produces a color that is characteristically slate gray and diffuse. An early sign of argyria is a grayish discoloration of the fingernails. Although in pronounced cases the appearance of the patient may be striking, there is no impairment to health.

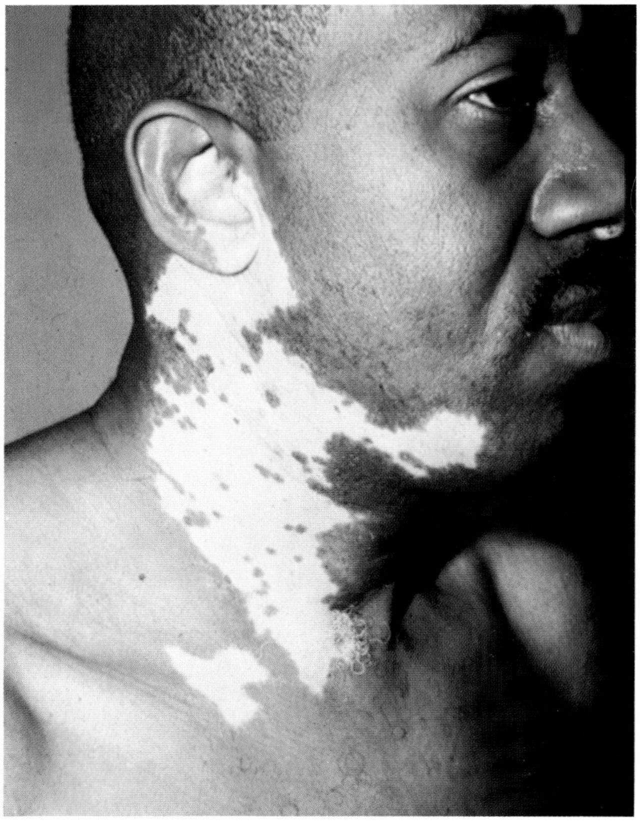

Figure 58. Vitiligo

DEPIGMENTATION

Two major types of cutaneous depigmentation include albinism and vitiligo. In albinism, the melanocytes lose the ability to produce melanin through a congenital defect in the tyrosinase enzyme system. The process may be complete (total lack of cutaneous pigment, pink irides) or partial (pibaldism). Albino skin is particularly susceptible to damage from solar irradiation, and the development of severe sunburn and later of keratosis and skin cancer is not uncommon. Ocular involvement produces photophobia and nystagmus, accompanied by poor vision. The disease is hereditary although the pattern of transmission varies.

YELLOW PIGMENTATION

Two general types of nonmelanin yellow, cutaneous pigmentation occur – jaundice and carotenosis. The clinical manifestations of jaundice are well known, including a generalized yellow or yellowish-brown or

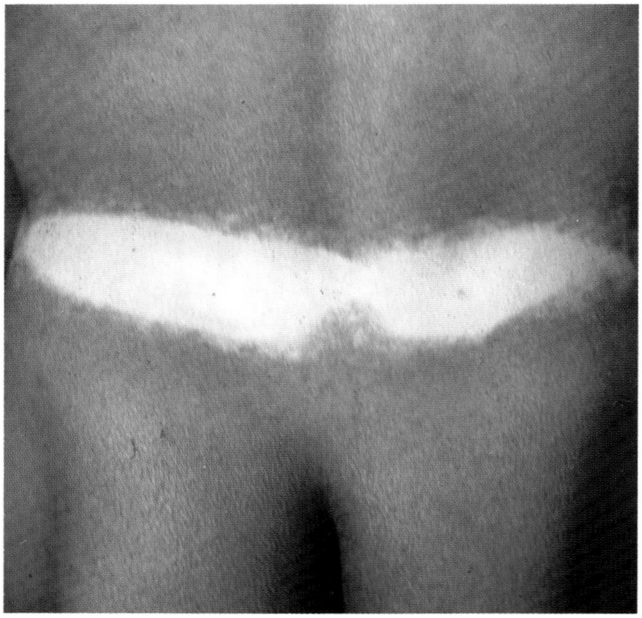

Figure 59. Depigmentation due to rubber at back midline

yellowish-green pigmentation. Frequently, jaundice is first detected in the sclera, which reflects a high affinity of bilirubin for elastic tissue.

Carotenosis results from elevated serum levels of carotene, a yellowish pigment which is a precursor of vitamin A.

Carotenemia may result from heavy intake of carotene-containing vegetables such as carrots and yellow squash or from defective vitamin A synthesis as postulated in diabetes mellitus.

Quinacrine hydrochloride produces a distinctive yellowish pigmentation of the skin, often after only a few days of use.

Diseases Presenting Smooth Nodules

Facial Lesions

REACTION PATTERN: In these diseases, the cutaneous pathologic process is localized to the dermis with little or no inflammatory process of the epidermis. The diagnosis in most instances must be confirmed by performing a biopsy. Morphologically, the lesions are raised above the skin surface.

INFILTRATIONS

Discoid Lupus Erythematosus: This condition involves women more frequently than men, and most lesions occur on the face, especially the nose, cheeks, and ears. The lesions are well-defined erythematous patches ranging from a few mm to 10 cm or more. During their evolution they develop adherent scales, with horny plugs extending into the pilosebaceous follicle openings. The surface of the lesions may be smooth or rough, depending upon the amount of scaling and plugging. In thickness, the lesions range from barely palpable plaques to thick nodular lesions. They evolve and regress over a period of time, several weeks to several months. Individual lesions heal with a thin white scar which has an elevated erythematous peripheral border. Old lesions may show considerable hyperpigmentation.

Lymphocytoma Cutis (Cutaneous Lymphoid Hyperplasia): In this disease process, women are affected more frequently than men, and lesions occur with greatest frequency on the face, especially the ear lobes and the nose. These lesions may be localized or may have generalized distribution. They evolve as smooth, dome-shaped papules or nodules within the skin, and there is usually slow enlargement of 3 to 5 cm. In consistency the lesions are firm or rubbery, and the color varies from yellowish-brown to reddish-blue to purple. Occasionally these lesions may regress spontaneously, usually with no scarring.

GRANULOMAS

Cutaneous Tuberculosis: There are several forms of secondary or reinfection cutaneous tuberculosis that produce clinically distinctive lesions on the face. Primary cutaneous tuberculosis generally does not affect the face and does not produce a distinctive lesion.

a. Lupus Vulgaris

This disease occurs in individuals with moderate or high-degree immunity to tuberculosis. Lesions occur most commonly on the face, and the onset is usually heralded by the appearance of a small, soft, yellowish-brown papule. This slowly extends peripherally to form

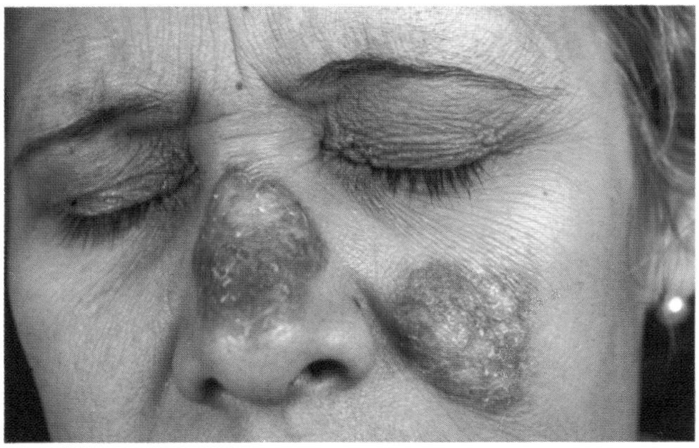

Figure 60. Lupus erythematosus

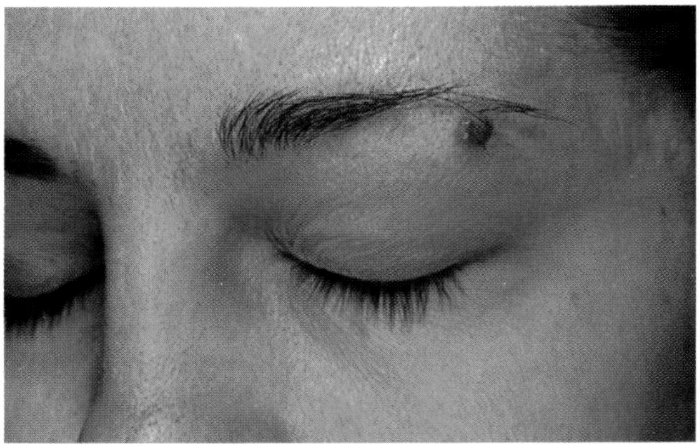

Figure 61. Lupus miliaris

an irregular plaque. Satellite lesions frequently develop, and upon compression with a glass slide there is a characteristic yellowish-brown nodular appearance, the so-called "apple jelly nodule." As the lesions extend there is central healing with considerable scar formation. The process ultimately may be extensive, and frequently at this stage squamous cell carcinoma may complicate lupus vulgaris.

b. Lupus Miliaris Disseminatus Faciei

These lesions occur on the face (of adults, usually) as a result of hematogenous dissemination. They appear as 1 to 2 cm discrete brownish papules distributed symmetrically over the periorbital, nasal, paranasal, and mental areas. The individual lesions are soft and translucent and usually resolve spontaneously over a 1 to 2 year period, leaving small pitted scars.

c. Papulonecrotic Tuberculid

This disease usually occurs on the face and extremities of young adults as a result of hematogenous dissemination. The individual lesions consist of deep-seated papules and nodules, which may become several centimeters in size. Characteristically, the lesions undergo early ulceration and heal with depressed pitted scarring. The course of the disease is shorter than that of lupus miliaris disseminatus faciei.

Leprosy: Facial nodules are characteristic of lepromatous leprosy. These lesions usually present as small erythematous macules, papules, or plaques which have poorly defined borders. The ears, nose, and chin are frequent areas of involvement, often with a diffuse thickening of the face, producing characteristic leonine facies. The lesions are infiltrated, have a smooth surface, and are usually symmetrically distributed. In color they may show erythema, hyperpigmentation, or hypopigmentation. Facial lesions of lepromatous leprosy are characteristically associated with nasal obstruction and epistaxis, signs of the consistent mucous membrane involvement of this disease.

Sarcoidosis: Cutaneous lesions of sarcoidosis commonly occur on the face and are more common in blacks than in whites. The lesions appear as discrete erythematous to yellowish-brown papules and nodules. The eyelids, ears, and nose are favored locations, and the lesions are usually symmetrically distributed. Infiltrated annular lesions and plaques also occur frequently.

Deep Fungal Infections: Deep fungal infections may produce facial nodules; this is especially true of blastomycosis. Skin lesions usually occur secondary to a pulmonary focus, and the most common mode of pre-

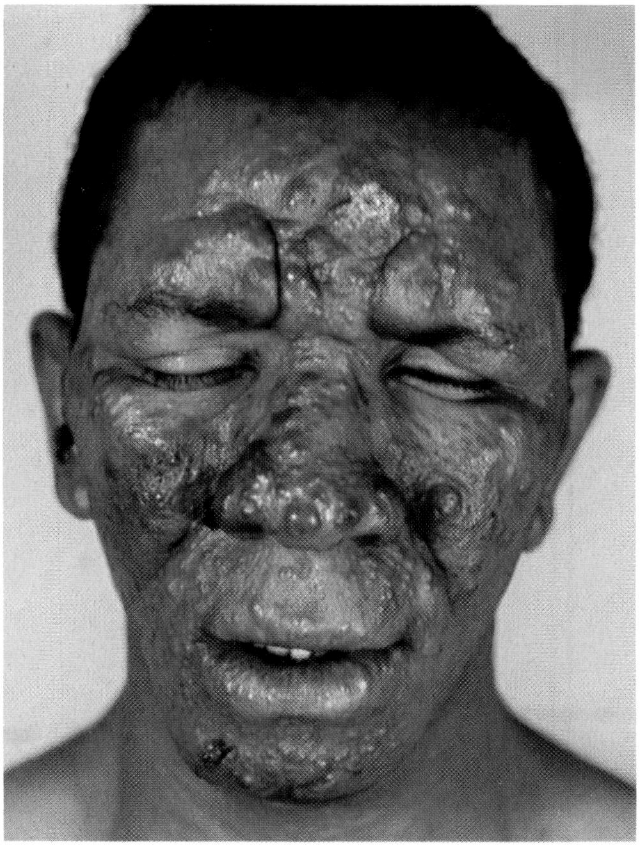

Figure 62. Lepromatous leprosy

sentation is a small, slowly enlarging papule. The surface of the lesion is frequently irregular, a manifestation of epithelial proliferation. As the lesion enlarges, the central area shows clearing with considerable scar formation. The peripheral border is frequently studded with pustules and has a verrucous configuration. With continuing enlargement, irregular serpiginous and gyrate configurations may result. These lesions will continue to enlarge relentlessly until treatment is initiated. With healing, there is considerable scar formation and frequent disfigurement.

Foreign-Body Granuloma: Foreign-body granulomas may occur on the face as well as elsewhere. Clinically, they do not have distinctive features and appear as nondescript papules or nodules with a verrucous surface. The diagnosis of foreign-body granulomas will depend upon the histopathological pattern. In some instances, the offending material may be demonstrated microscopically.

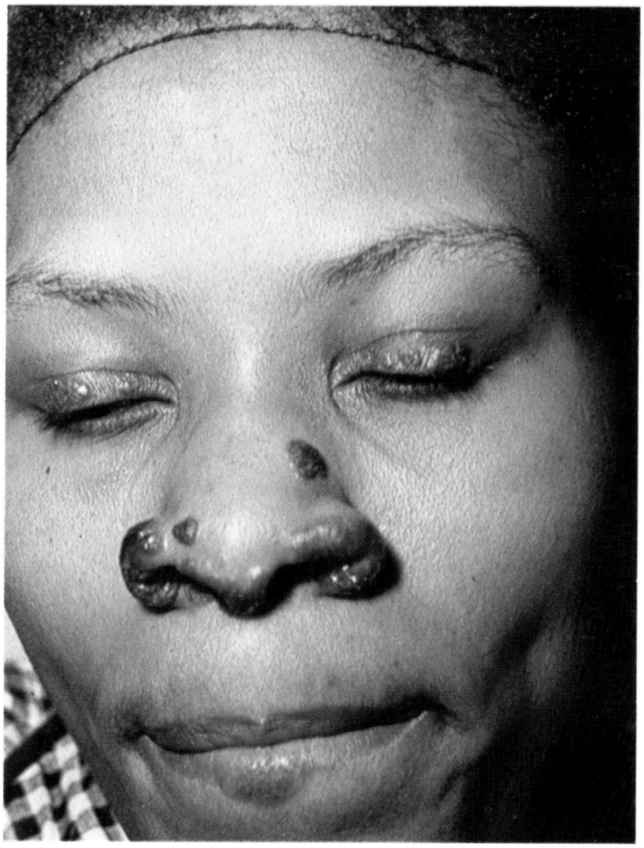

Figure 63. Sarcoidosis

DEGENERATIVE DISEASES

Amyloidosis: Facial nodules occur in primary systemic amyloidosis. The lesions are of variable size and have a yellowish, waxy appearance with a rubbery consistency. Because of the blood vessels' involvement, lesions frequently show associated hemorrhage secondary to palpation or manipulation.

Xanthomas: Xanthomas occur as soft, firm, yellowish papules, nodules, or plaques. Xanthelasma is the most characteristic xanthoma of the face and appears as symmetrical, soft, yellowish-brown papules near the inner canthi of the eyes. The upper lids are frequently involved but the condition may affect both lids.

BENIGN TUMORS

Juvenile Xanthogranuloma: Juvenile xanthogranuloma represents a benign histiocytic infiltration of the skin

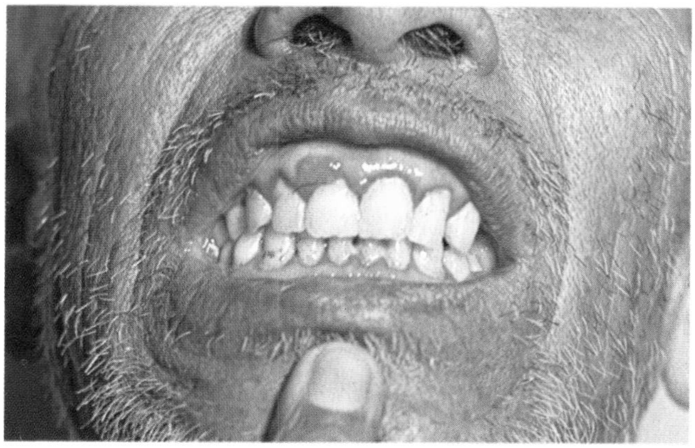

Figure 64. Amyloidosis

occurring primarily in children during the first months of life. It most frequently involves the scalp, face, trunk, and extremities and occurs in crops with an irregular distribution pattern. The individual lesions are round to oval, sharply defined, firm, and reddish to yellow papules of several millimeters to 1 cm in size. After several months the lesions usually involute spontaneously. Although juvenile xanthogranuloma is usually confined to the skin, it may occur elsewhere, e.g., the eye.

Adenoma Sebaceum: Approximately 60%-70% of patients with tuberous sclerosis have associated lesions of adenoma sebaceum. The lesions occur as firm, discrete, yellowish to erythematous papules of variable size, and some may show surface telangiectasia. Favored areas include the nasolabial fold, cheeks, and chin. The onset occurs between the ages of 5 and 10, and at puberty the lesions may become extensive and exuberant. Adenoma sebaceum is actually a misnomer, as the lesion histologically is a fibrovascular hyperplasia.

Pyogenicum Granuloma: Pyogenic granulomas usually occur as single, exuberant, papular lesions on the face with a special predilection around the mouth. The lesions appear vascular and show varying degrees of erythema from bright red to bluish-black. The surface is thin and may be eroded with crusting. Younger (newer) lesions may have a raspberry appearance with verrucous configuration. The lesions range in size from Several millimeters to 1 cm and may be attached to the underlying skin by a short stalk. Spontaneous bleeding is not infrequent.

Trichoepithelioma: Trichoepitheliomas usually appear at puberty as small, multiple, translucent papules and nodules symmetrically distributed over the face. They occur frequently over the eyelids and in the nasolabial folds and range in color from pink to yellowish while presenting a fine surface telangiectasia. The lesions usually show a dominant inheritance pattern, although a single lesion may occur without any hereditary pattern.

MALIGNANT TUMORS

Basal Cell Carcinoma: Basal cell carcinoma, the most-frequent malignant tumor of the skin, appears as numerous different types, often as a variably sized, round to oval papule or nodule on the face. The lesion has a translucent hue and may show surface telangiectasia. With enlargement, the central area may become depressed or ulcerated, although the periphery is maintained as an elevated advancing border. Basal cell carcinoma is locally destructive with continuous autonomous growth.

Squamous Cell Carcinoma: Squamous cell carcinoma occurs with greatest frequency on the face and favors areas such as the ears, nose, and lower lip. The lesion appears as a gradually enlarging, firm papule with a heaped-up border and a verrucous center. On enlargement, central ulceration is common. Squamous cell carcinoma is locally destructive and continues to grow autonomously. Metastases may occur.

Malignant Lymphomas: Malignant lymphomas may affect the skin anytime during the course of the disease and may actually precede the onset of clinical signs. The lesions usually present as slowly enlarging, firm, smooth nodules or plaques. The color ranges from bright erythema to a dusky reddish-blue hue. Large lesions may ultimately ulcerate.

Lesions on Legs

Nodular lesions occur on the legs in a number of different diseases. In some cases, the distinction among the various diseases, both clinically and histopathologically, is indeterminate, so a precise classification is not possible. REACTION PATTERN: In these diseases, the cutaneous pathologic process is localized to the dermis with little or no inflammatory process of the epidermis. The diagnosis in most instances must be confirmed by performing a biopsy. Morphologically, the lesions are raised above the skin surface.

ERYTHEMA NODOSUM

Erythema nodosum appears as a reaction pattern involving the anterior surface of the legs of young women. The cutaneous lesions are frequently heralded by a simultaneous appearance of malaise, fever, and arthralgia. The lesions appear as symmetrically distributed, tender, warm, erythematous, and deep-seated nodules. They usually occur in successive crops over a period of several days to two weeks and then slowly involute. During involution, there is a characteristic color change from erythema through varying shades of blue and brown, which resembles the resolution of an ecchymosis. Lesions of erythema nodosum may also involve the arms and the body in addition to the legs. This reaction pattern may appear without preceding demonstrable cause as a secondary manifestation of bacterial or fungal infection, drug reaction, sarcoidosis, tuberculosis, or other disease.

ERYTHEMA INDURATUM

This process is characterized by recurrent eruption of ill-defined nodules affecting the posterior aspect of the legs in young and middle-aged women and appears to be precipitated by cold weather. The lesions begin as subcutaneous nodules, with gradual extension to the

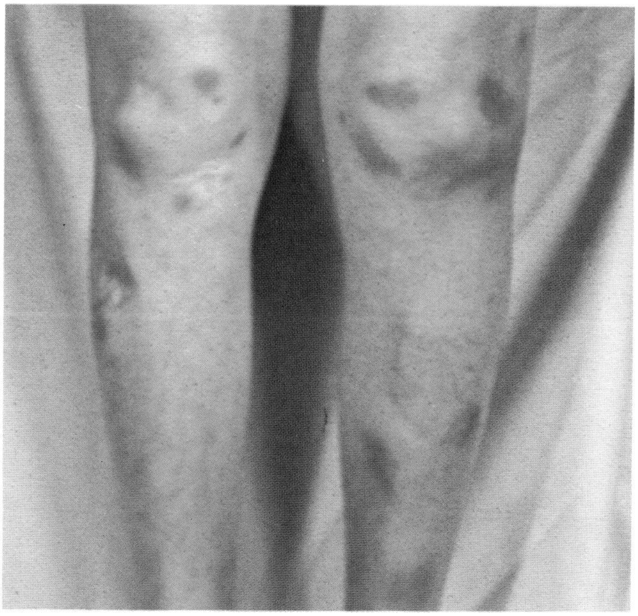

Figure 65. Erythema nodosum

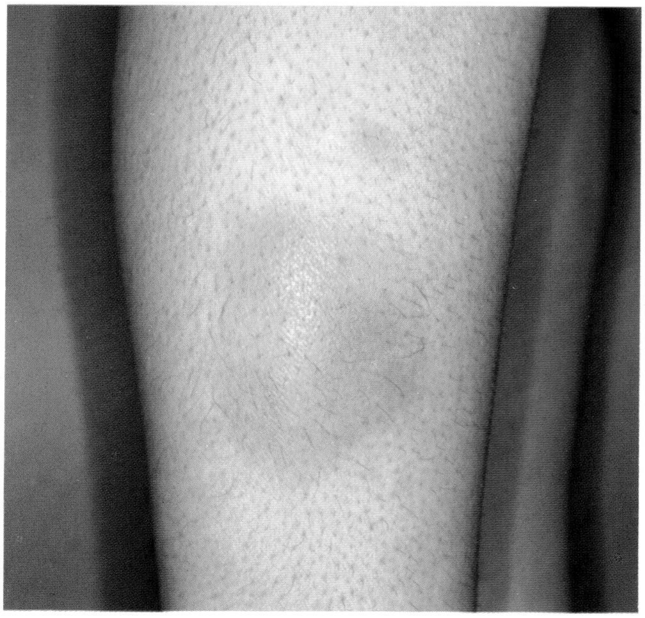

Figure 66. Erythema nodosum

surface. Necrosis and ulceration occur with the ultimate production of an atrophic scar. Over a number of months the condition heals. In the past, a tuberculous etiology was reported for many cases but usually could not be verified. Like erythema nodosum, erythema induratum is believed to be a reaction pattern involving the vessels in the deeper dermis and subcutaneous layer.

NODULAR VASCULITIS

Nodular vasculitis commonly occurs posterolaterally on the legs of young and middle-aged women. The lesions begin as small subcutaneous nodules and grow into larger nodules and plaques. The lesions are often tender, painful, and may be ulcerated with slow resolution of the process, and scarring invariably occurs. The distinction between nodular vasculitis and erythema induratum is not well drawn.

WEBER-CHRISTIAN DISEASE
(Relapsing febrile nodular nonsuppurative panniculitis)

This disease is characterized by recurrent crops of subcutaneous inflammatory nodules, usually occurring on the thighs, legs, and buttocks of women 20-40 years of age. The individual lesions are initially dull red, edematous and tender, and may be mobile or attached to the underlying skin. Over a period of weeks the lesions gradually resolve, resulting in permanently depressed areas with atrophy and hyperpigmentation. Constitutional symptoms vary, but anorexia, fatigue, and fever are quite frequent. Subcutaneous fat throughout the body may also be involved in Weber-Christian disease.

PRETIBIAL MYXEDEMA

This disease usually occurs in patients with hyperthyroidism and frequently has its onset following thyroidectomy. The lesions occur primarily over the anterior tibial areas and initially may be papular, with ultimate enlargement into broad plaques. The fully developed plaques show a nonpitting induration with follicular accentuation due to edema. The color ranges from normal skin color to a dull erythematous or yellowish hue. The process is chronic without spontaneous resolution.

PANNICULITIS

Panniculitis is a reaction pattern of varying etiology and is characterized by subcutaneous nodules within the body fat. Frequently, the extremities are involved and an individual lesion may or may not be tender. Some cases are associated with constitutional symptoms, whereas others are not. The lesions vary in size, number, location, and duration. In some conditions the process may be relapsing; in others it may be migratory.

POLYARTERITIS NODOSA

Skin lesions are involved in approximately 20% of patients with polyarteritis nodosa and in males more fre-

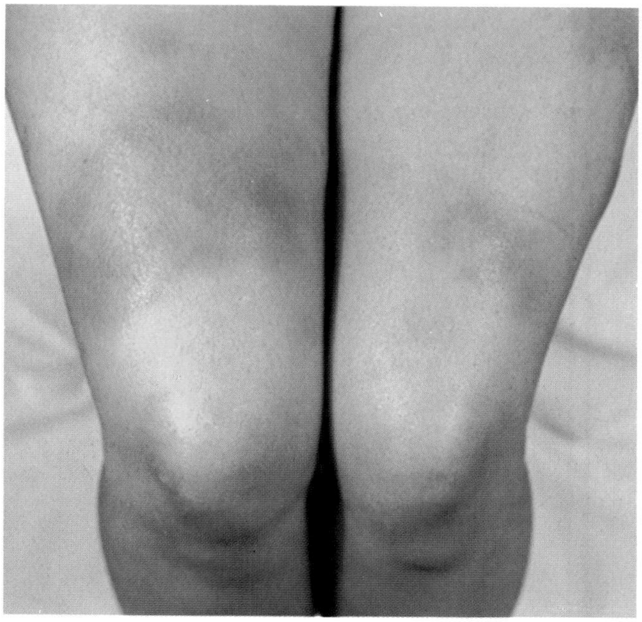

Figure 67. Weber-Christian disease

quently than females. Prior to the onset of skin lesions, there is usually evidence of systemic disease with fever, malaise, weight loss, and evidence of renal, pulmonary, or cardiovascular disease. The onset may consist of relatively acute lesions with urticaria, erythema, or purpura. However, the protean lesion may be macular, papular, or vesiculobullous. Ulceration is common, and a characteristic finding is the appearance of nodules along the course of superficial arteries, especially in the lower extremities. Individual lesions may persist for several days to months and are usually tender, with the color ranging from flesh to bright erythema.

LEUKEMIC INFILTRATIONS

Although the most-frequent skin lesions associated with leukemia are nonspecific (eczematous eruptions, zoster, purpura, and exfoliative dermatitis), specific leukemic infiltrates produce nodular cutaneous lesions. These commonly appear on the face and head but may occur on the lower extremities or elsewhere. The lesions are variable in size. The nodules are firm, smooth, and dome-shaped, with an erythematous to violaceous hue.

PANCREATIC FAT NECROSIS

Patients with acute pancreatitis may develop scattered subcutaneous nodules, which represent localized areas of fat necrosis. The lesions are usually multiple, erythematous in color, and range in size from 1 to 2 cm. Although the legs are frequently the areas of involvement, the process may be more extensive. The individual lesions may or may not be tender. The underlying abnormality is thought to be the release of lipolytic enzymes into the blood from the damaged pancreas.

Cutaneous Atrophies

REACTION PATTERN: Atrophy or loss of tissue substance may involve the epidermis, dermis, or both, and fibrosis may or may not be present. Morphologically, the skin lesion will be depressed with or without palpable fibrosis.

LINEAR ATROPHY (Striae distensae)

This condition occurs most frequently in women following pregnancy and consists of stripes of thinned and slightly wrinkled skin over the abdomen, breasts, and thighs. Initially, the stripes may have a purplish cast, but often become whitish when they are fully developed. These lesions are also seen in obese individuals and are noticeable following weight loss. The skin over these lesions looks thin, and a microscopic examination reveals a thinned epidermis with flattened rete ridges. The dermis also is thinned and the number of elastic fibers is diminished in some areas.

Linear atrophy occurs in Cushing disease, in the cushingoid syndrome of steroid overdosage, not infrequently during puberty (in the absence of obesity), and has been induced locally by frequent application of a topical corticosteroid ointment. Atrophy appears to be induced as a response to the presence of increased amounts of corticosteroids, physiologically in pregnancy, pathologically in Cushing disease, or iatrogenically in response to steroid therapy.

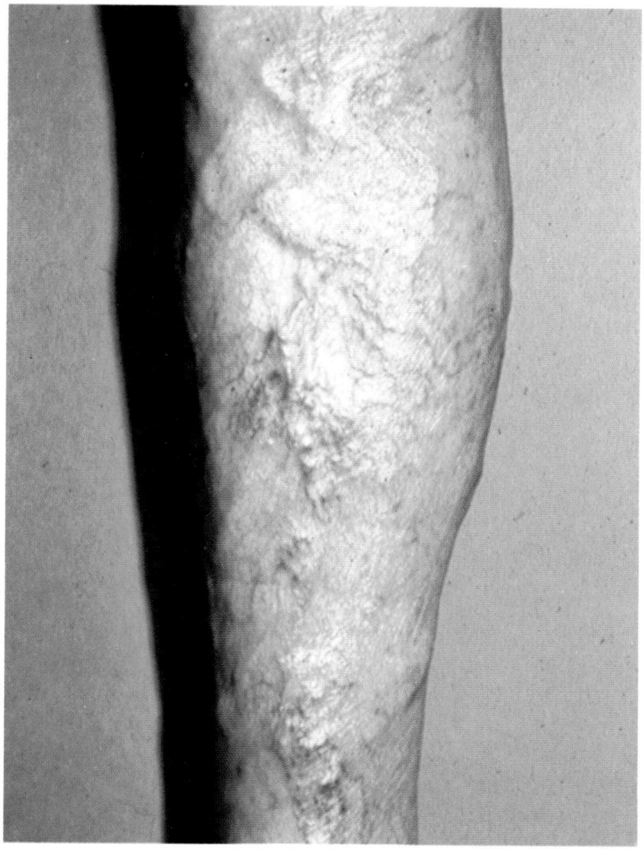

Figure 68. Acrodermatitis chronica atrophicans

MORPHEA

Morphea is often called localized scleroderma. The lesion begins as a round or elongated violaceous patch. Over a period of time, the patch will enlarge and the center becomes pale white or yellowish and is quite firm. After months or years, the violet color is lost and the patch is uniformly pale and hard to the touch. It also becomes depressed below the level of the surrounding normal skin.

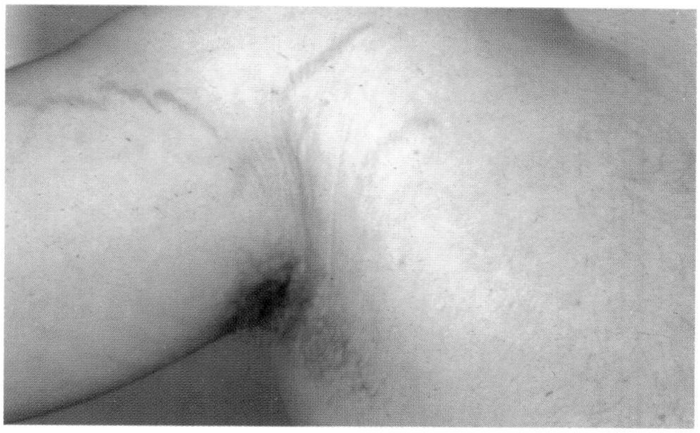

Figure 69. Linear atrophy

Figure 70. (top) Morphea

Figure 71. (middle) Senile elastosis

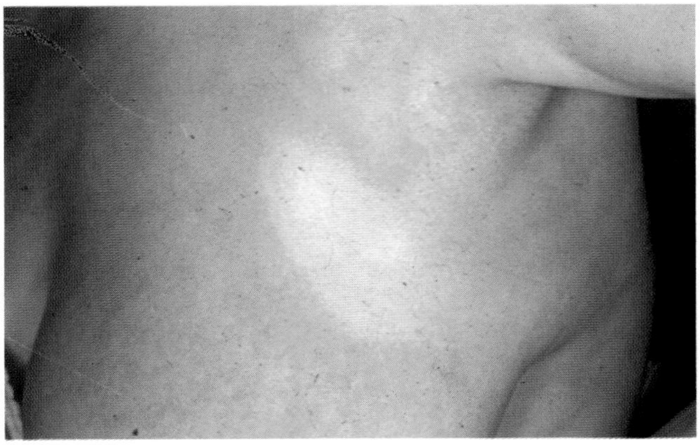

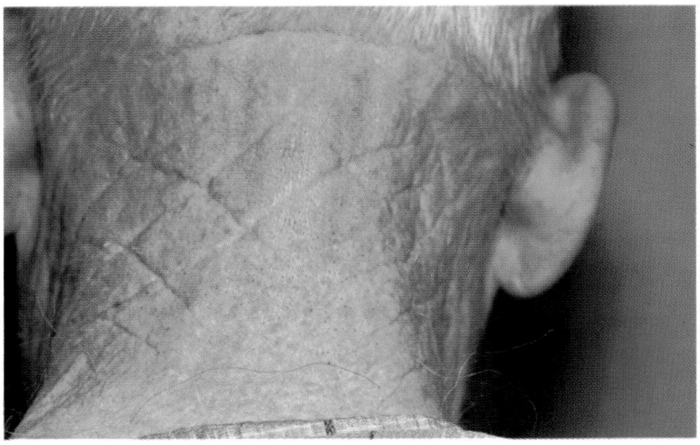

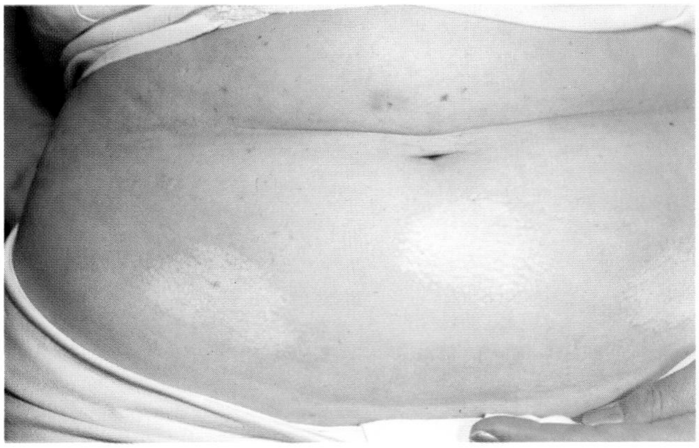

Figure 72. Lichen sclerosus

A microscopic examination usually demonstrates a more-or-less normal epidermis. The dermis, however, will show swelling and edema of the collagen fibers, absence of sebaceous glands and hair follicles, and some replacement of subcutaneous fat by collagen.

Prognosis is good. No treatment is indicated.

SENILE ATROPHY

In senile atrophy, the epidermis and the elastic and collagen fibers of the dermis shrink. Clinically, there is dryness and thinning of the skin, loss of elasticity, and wrinkling.

LICHEN SCLEROSUS ET ATROPHICUS

This condition is an example of epidermal atrophy. Clinically, it starts as whitish, irregular, flat-topped papules with a central depression (delling) and later is seen as white, depressed lesions. The lesions usually occur on genitalia and are probably hormonal, as they occur in young girls before adolescence and in postmenopausal women. The male counterpart is balanitis xerotica obliterans in which the glans penis is shriveled, white, and glossy, and the meatus is stenosed.

POIKILODERMA VASCULARE ATROPHICANS

This disease is clinically characterized by telangiectasia, pigmentation, and atrophy. It resembles x-ray dermatitis and epidermal atrophy. The disease may be a precursor to the lymphomas.

DISCOID LUPUS ERYTHEMATOSUS

Clinically, this disease presents an erythematous border surrounding adherent scales with follicular plugging; fibrosis is usually palpable. Lesions appear most commonly on exposed areas, especially the face.

IDIOPATHIC ATROPHODERMA (Pasini-Pierini)

Clinical characteristics of this disease are depressed

lesions with sharp borders and hyperpigmented bases with no palpable fibrosis, but the disease is thought to be a variant of morphea. Lesions of this disease usually appear on the trunk and back.

MACULAR ATROPHY

A wrinkled surface with little resistance to palpation (falling in sensation) is characteristic of this disease. Macular atrophy is thought to be a variant of neurofibromatosis.

DIFFUSE IDIOPATHIC ATROPHY
(Acrodermatitis chronica atrophicans)

Clinically, this disease is characterized by a cigarette-paper-thin skin with vessels that are conspicuous because of the thinness of the overlying epidermis. Distribution is mainly confined to the extremities, rarely on the face.

OTHER

Other causes of atrophy include icthyosis, congenital icthyosiform erythroderma, radiodermatitis, scleroderma, addict's scars, atrophy following herpes zoster, neurotic excoriations, or intradermal injections of insulin or steroids. In most instances of atrophy of the skin, the distribution pattern is not distinctive.

Acneform Eruptions

REACTION PATTERN: Comedones, papules, pustules, and cysts are predominant on the face and, to a lesser extent, on the back and chest. Histologically, there is plugging of the pilosebaceous unit, with surrounding acute and chronic inflammation.

ACNE VULGARIS

Acne is characterized clinically by the appearance of blackheads (open comedones), whiteheads (closed comedones), papules, pustules, and cysts occurring on the face and, to a lesser extent, on the back and chest.

The occurrence of acne depends upon the development of sebaceous glands. The sites of pathologic change, however, are not the glands themselves, but rather are the follicles into which they empty secretion (sebum). At puberty, sebaceous glands undergo enlargement as a result of hormonal stimulation (androgens).

The inflammatory lesions of acne arise as a result of

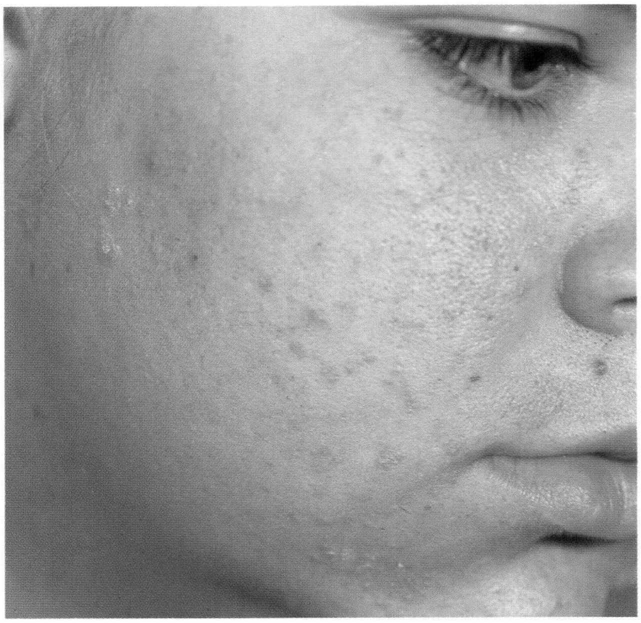

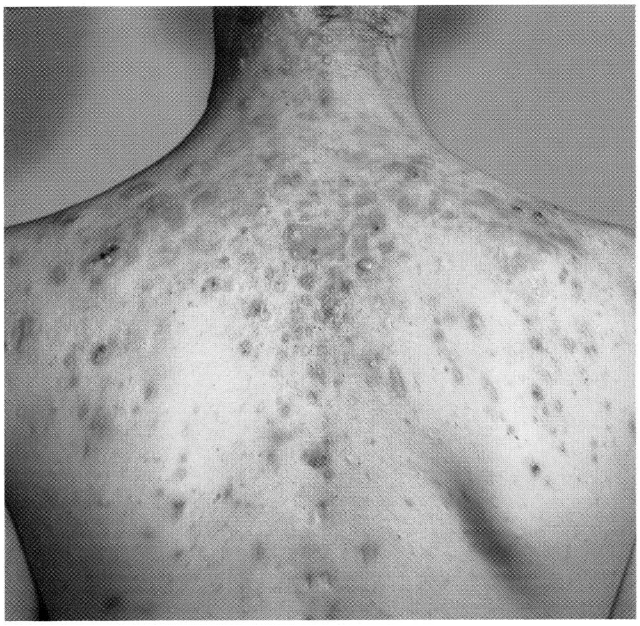

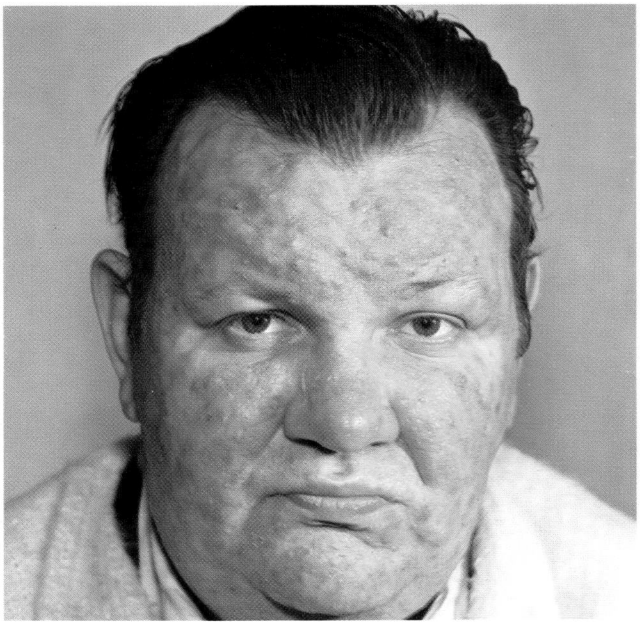

Figure 73. Severe acne with scarring

Figure 74. (top) Mild acne with comedones

Figure 75. (bottom) Rosacea

the irritant action of sebum, which escapes into the dermis through breaks in the follicular walls. These lesions may arise either in normal appearing follicles or from preexisting whiteheads.

ROSACEA

This disease is associated with hyperplasia of sebaceous glands, and increased vascularity and vasodilatation in the middle third of the face. Clinically, these are papular, pustular, and telangiectatic lesions.

Other acneform lesions are caused by drug usage: In these acneform lesions, comedones are usually not observed. The drugs most commonly involved are iodides, bromides, isonicotinic hydrazide (INH), some anticonvulsive agents, corticotropin (ACTH), corticosteroids, and androgens in high doses.

CHEMICALS: Chemicals such as oils, tars, pesticides, or medicinal agents may be the cause of acneform eruptions.

TREATMENT: Topically, excess oil is removed by:

1. Cleansing of the skin
2. Drying lotions
   a. Most acne lotions contain resorcin and sulfur in various combinations and concentrations
   b. Vleminckx solution (sulfurated lime)
   c. Carbon dioxide slush applications

Systemic therapy includes measures to control infection and slow down the sebum production.

1. Antibiotics (tetracyclines preferred)
2. Hormones (estrogen-progestin combinations in girls)

Vascular Reactions
(Vasculitis)

The blood vessels of the skin (the dermal capillary loops, small veins and arteries in the upper or lower dermis) are the primary target tissue.

REACTION PATTERN: Clinically, vasculitis is manifested in several somewhat overlapping patterns.

The mildest form of vascular reaction is simple vasodilatation. This is recognized clinically as *erythema*. Histologically, there are only engorged blood vessels.

In a less-mild form, when in addition to vasodilatation the fluid part of the blood passes through the vessel wall, the condition is called *urticaria* and is clinically recognizable as a wheal, with redness and itching. Histologically, there are dilated blood vessels and evidence of edema.

In a moderate form, the blood vessels are damaged so that the formed elements of the blood–primarily the erythrocytes–are extravasated. This is recognized clinically as *purpura* and can be differentiated from transient vasodilatation (erythema) or permanent vasodilatation (telangiectasia) by the simple observation that the red color cannot be erased by pressure with a glass slide (diascopy). Histologically, there are extravasated blood cells, inflammatory cells, and dilated blood vessels.

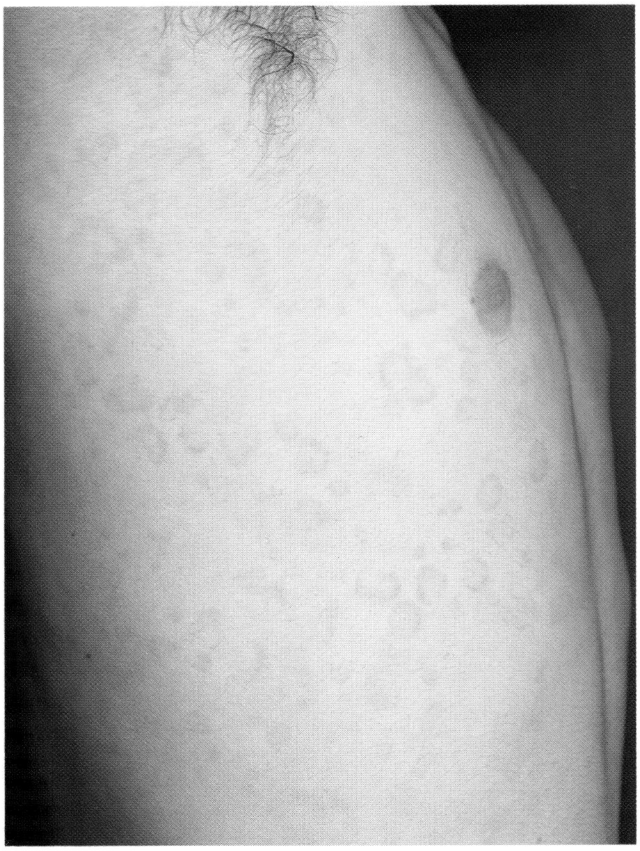

Figure 76. Erythema annulare

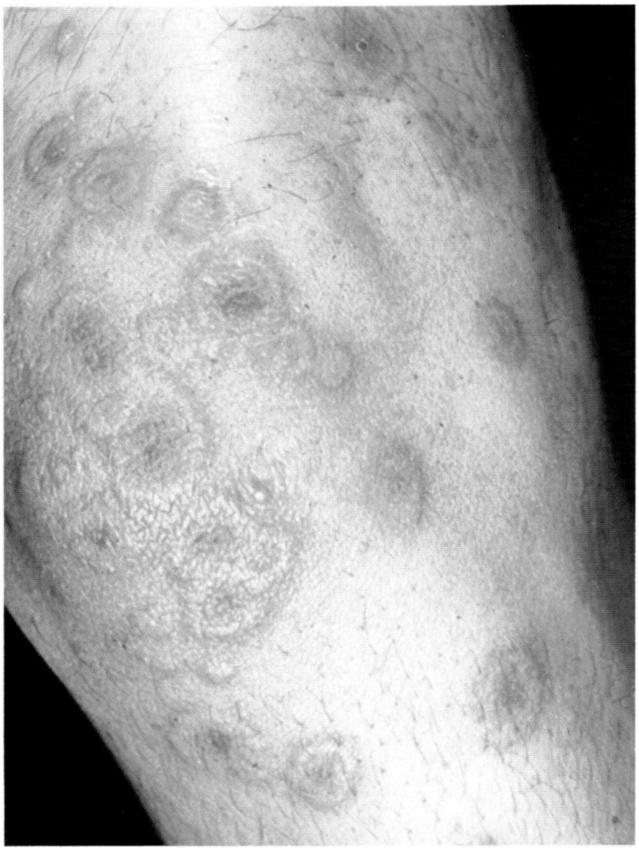

Figure 77. Erythema multiforme (iris lesions)

In a severe form, the blood vessels are inflamed in varying degrees and there is localized cutaneous necrosis. These may be smooth, inflammatory nodules along the blood vessels. The condition is loosely called *vasculitis*.

The clinical characteristics are redness and tenderness, sometimes followed by ulceration and atrophy, leaving sharply punched-out, depressed scars. Nodules may occur when the deep blood vessels are involved. Histologically, arteriolar damage and fibrinoid changes occur. There may also be a leukocytic reaction, inflammation of vessel walls, thrombosis, tissue necrosis (infarction), and involvement of the deep blood vessels of the dermis and fat, causing panniculitis.

In its most-severe form, the vascular damage can be so extensive as to produce massive gangrene of the skin and adjacent tissues.

ERYTHEMA

Evanescent erythema is frequently seen in infectious diseases and rheumatic fever. The redness of the skin is produced by congestion of the capillaries, which may result from a variety of causes, including allergies.

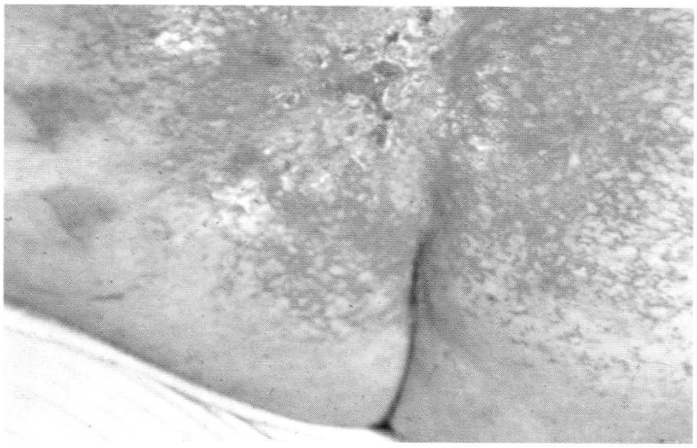

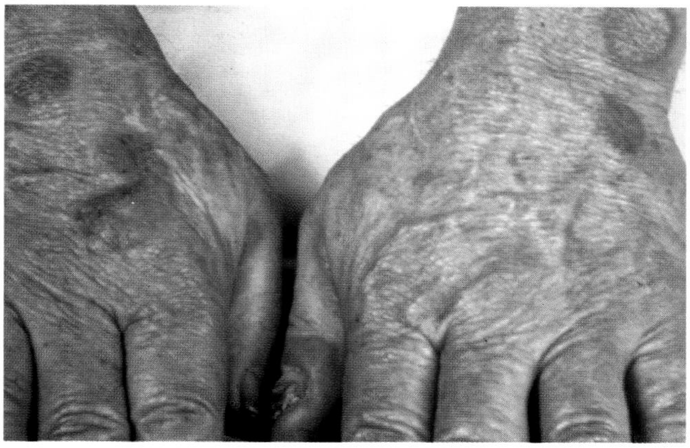

Figure 78. (top) X-ray dermatitis

Figure 79. (bottom) Erythema elevatum diutinum

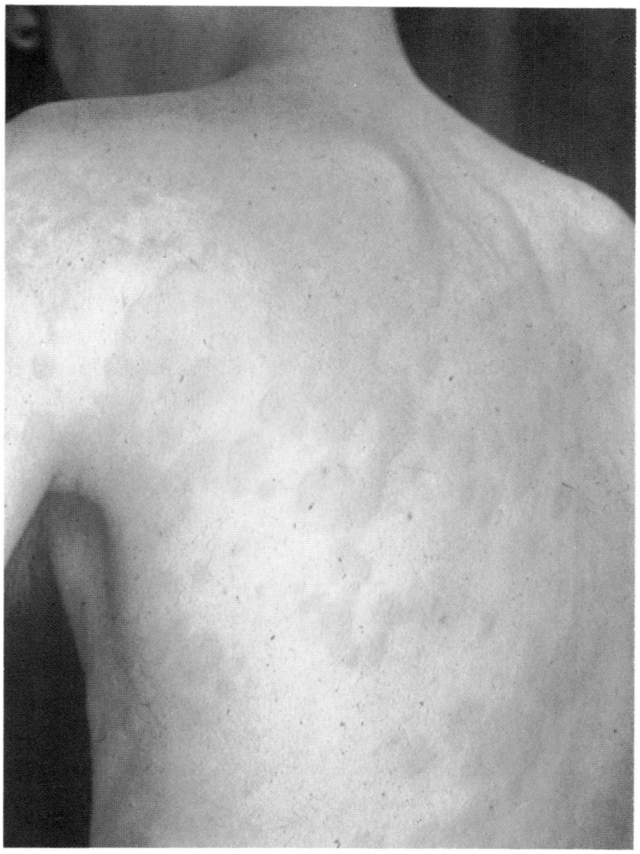

Figure 80. Urticaria

URTICARIA

Urticarias are produced by release of substances that act on capillaries (histamine, bradykinin, neurohumors) to produce capillary permeability. Chemicals or physical factors may cause the release of these vasoactive substances. Urticarias may also be caused by circulating antibodies (reagins) reacting with antigen.

Inciting agents can be:

1. Allergens: drugs, food, inhalants
2. Nonallergenic substances
   a. Drugs: morphine, codeine
   b. Cholinergic urticaria
   c. Cold and solar urticaria
3. External agents (allergenic in some instances)
   a. Insect bites
   b. Dermographism
   c. Darier sign in urticaria pigmentosa (mastocytosis)
4. Systemic diseases
   a. Parasitic, bacterial, viral, and fungal infections
   b. Neoplastic diseases and lymphoma-leukemia
   c. Urticaria pigmentosa
   d. Autoimmune diseases (lupus erythematosus, rheumatoid arthritis, etc)

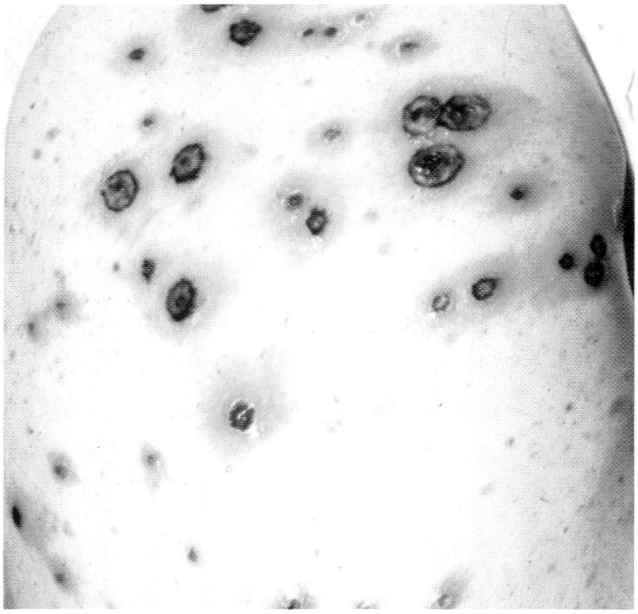

Figure 81. Necrotizing varicella

PURPURA

Purpura is essentially a hemorrhage into the skin or mucous membranes. The various terms employed, such as petechia, ecchymoses, purpura, hematoma, black and blue spots, vibex, and suffusion are quantitative and qualitative descriptions of this hemorrhage. Purpura may be the result of a variety of mechanisms, such as the following:

1. Disturbances in clotting mechanism
   a. Von Willebrand disease – An inherited defect of the vascular endothelium.
   b. Hemophilia–Disorder of males, transmitted as X chromosomal recessive traits. Deficiency of antihemophilial factor (factor VIII).
2. Quantitative or qualitative changes of platelets
   a. Thrombocytopenic purpura, primary
   b. Thrombocytopenic purpura, secondary (anemias, leukemias, disorders associated with splenomegaly, infections, drugs, radiation, metabolic and collagen diseases)
3. Increased permeability of the capillary wall
   a. Anaphylactoid purpura (Schönlein-Henoch disease)
   b. Scurvy
   c. Pigmented purpuric eruptions (Schamberg disease)
4. Dysproteinemic purpura
   a. Multiple myeloma
   b. Waldenstrom macroglobulinemia
5. External
   a. Trauma
   b. Contact dermatitis

Figure 82. Acute parapsoriasis

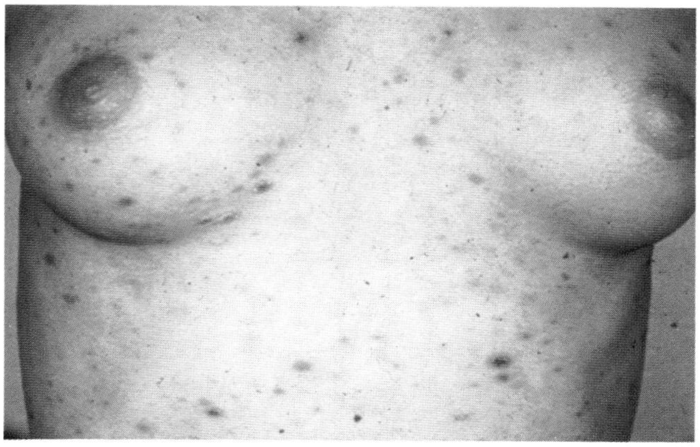

NODULES (vasculitis)

An example of the mildest form of vasculitis is anaphylactoid purpura (Schönlein-Henoch). A variant of this is nodular allergic disease. The clinical appearance includes petechial, hemorrhagic vesicles which heal with an eschar or ulceration and subsequent atrophy of the skin. Involvement of the deep vessels produces inflammatory nodules in the skin. The accompanying signs of generalized vasculitis are frequently present: involvement of the kidney, liver, lungs, central nervous system, and gastrointestinal tract. While this form of vasculitis may be due to drugs

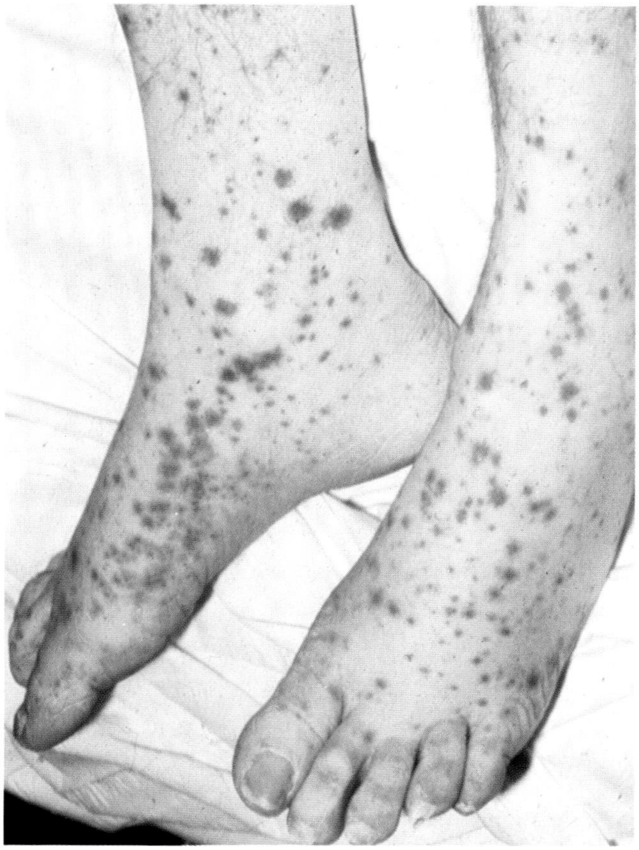

Figure 83. Purpura due to nafcillin, patient with thrombocytopenia

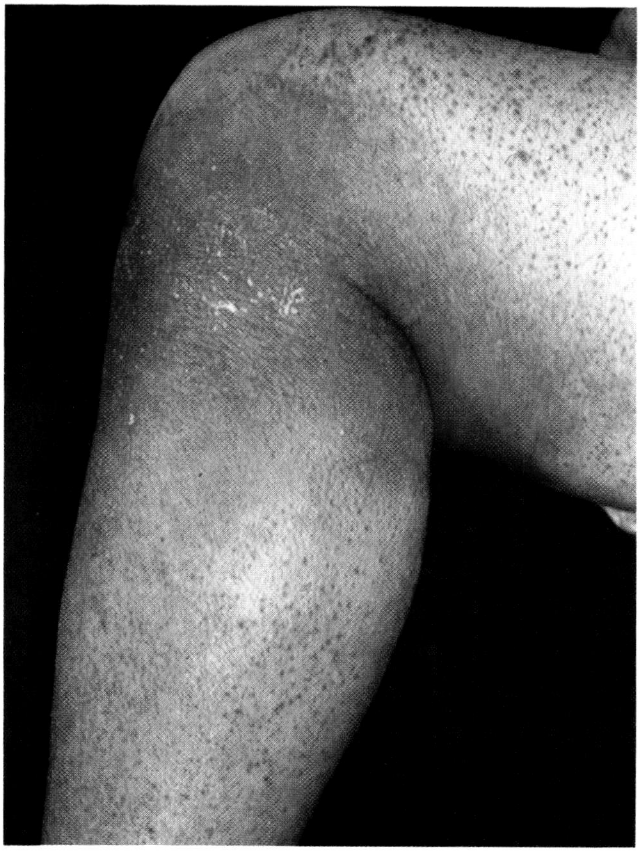

Figure 84. Frostbite purpura

or bacterial infection, its presence suggests an underlying disease such as:

Acute parapsoriasis: Onset is acute with papules or vesicles; later the lesions become crusted, leaving residual scars. The basic lesion is a vasculitis, and the disease must be differentiated from varicella.

Erythema Nodosum: This disorder is a symptom complex affecting the blood vessels, and it may be caused by many factors—the most prominent are streptococcal infection, drugs, sarcoidosis, infectious mononucleosis, and tuberculosis. Clinically, there are red, tender nodules present, usually on the tibial surfaces of the legs. The lesions occur in crops that last approximately two weeks; while healing, the lesions resemble old bruises. The pathology is a vasculitis of the deep vessels and an inflammatory infiltrate extending into the fat (panniculitis).

Nodular Vasculitis: Erythematous nodules occur usually on the calves in adult women. Histologically, there is a vasculitis of the deep vessels.

Periarteritis Nodosa: Medium and smaller arteries are affected, not only in the skin but in other organs as well. Clinically, painful nodules may develop that become necrotic. While the mechanism of action is unknown, it may be an allergic reaction to drugs or infectious agents. Histologically, the medium and small arteries show necrosis with surrounding inflammation and hemorrhage. Thrombosis and infarction are often present.

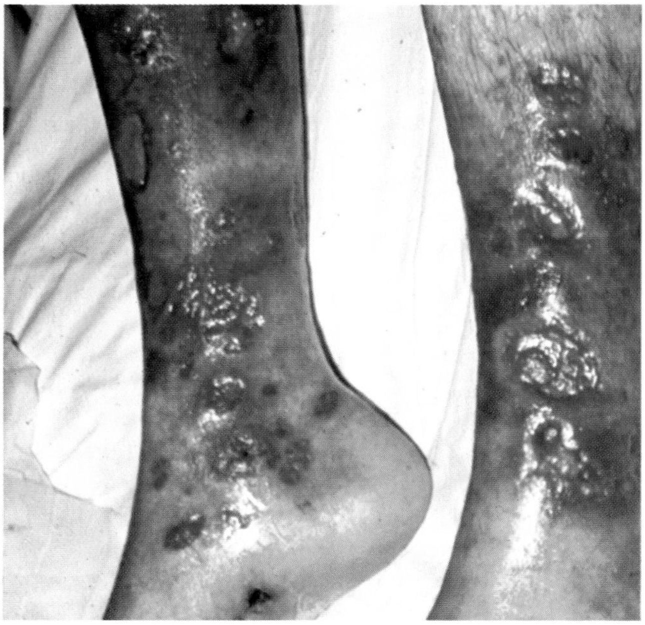

Figure 85. Periarteritis nodosa

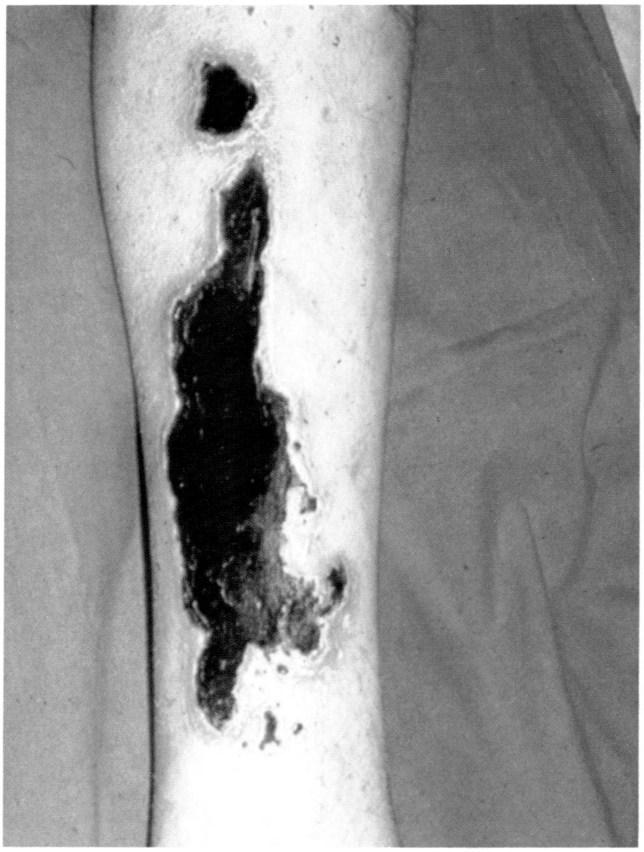

Figure 86. Cutaneous gangrene associated with rheumatoid arthritis

Alopecias

Loss of scalp hairs may occur at several levels: (1) distally on the hair shaft several mm above the surface in hair breakage of trichotillomania or following exessive exposure to chemicals—cold-wave solutions, bleaches, hair straighteners, and dyes; (2) at the follicular orifices in tinea capitis; (3) complete loss, including the hair bulbs, as in thallium poisoning or secondary syphilis. The hairs may be lost in localized patches or diffusely over the entire scalp. In extreme alopecia areata of the universalis type, eyelashes, eyebrows, beard, axillary and pubic hairs as well as scalp hairs are lost. The hair loss may be accompanied by scar formation as in discoid lupus erythematosus and morphea or may be associated with nodules as in sarcoidosis and carcinomas. Generally, the differential diagnosis of alopecias is best considered as scars or tumors rather than as alopecias.

NONCICATRICIAL ALOPECIAS

In male pattern baldness, the scalp hairs of the central area of the head change to vellus hairs or are lost entirely. Such hair loss is genetically controlled. Alternatively, hairs may be absent from infancy in the various congenital diseases.

Alopecia areata occurs spontaneously as sharply demarcated bald patches. In the early stages, one finds short, broken hairs tapering to a narrow base at the follicular orifices—the so-called "exclamation point" hairs. In most adults the hairs regrow spontaneously within a year. Occasionally, the hair loss progresses to involve the entire scalp.

Tinea capitis (nonkerion variety) produces a localized or an irregular alopecia with hair stubs frequently visible as black dots in the follicular orifices. A greenish fluorescence is frequently seen in Wood light examination.

Secondary syphilis most frequently produces an irregular alopecia, leaving a "moth eaten" appearance, although diffuse hair loss may occur.

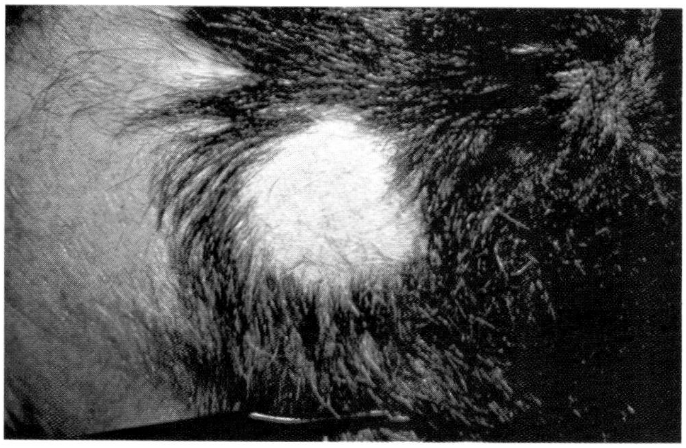

Figure 87. Alopecia areata

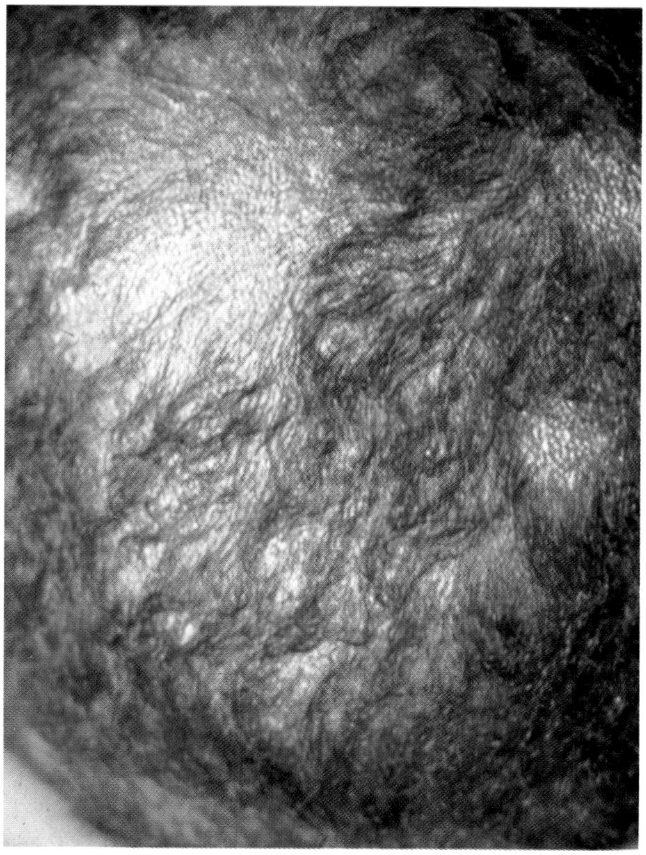

Figure 88. Tinea tonsurans

Figure 89. Secondary syphilis

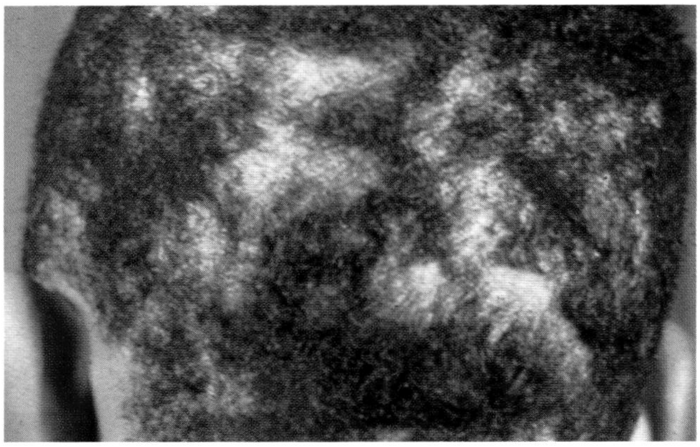

Mechanical hair breakage from excessive chemicals or from twisting or pulling of the hairs (trichotillomania) almost always leaves short lengths of hairs in the bald areas, and the base is uninflamed.

Alopecia mucinosa is a focal alopecia with a palpably infiltrated base due to accumulation of mucopolysaccharides around the hair follicle.

Pseudopelade in the early stages shows little if any fibrosis, and the alopecia occurs in irregular patches. Many of the hairs can be removed with minimal traction and the hair root is covered with a fine membrane-like sheath. In later stages extensive fibrosis may be apparent.

Diffuse hair loss may occur in many systemic diseases such as systemic lupus erythematosus, bacterial or viral infections with high fevers, chemical poisons (thallium), or with dicoumarol or antimetabolites. It may also occur secondary to pregnancy. Even in the absence of demonstrable systemic disease, diffuse hair loss may be associated with exfoliative dermatitis.

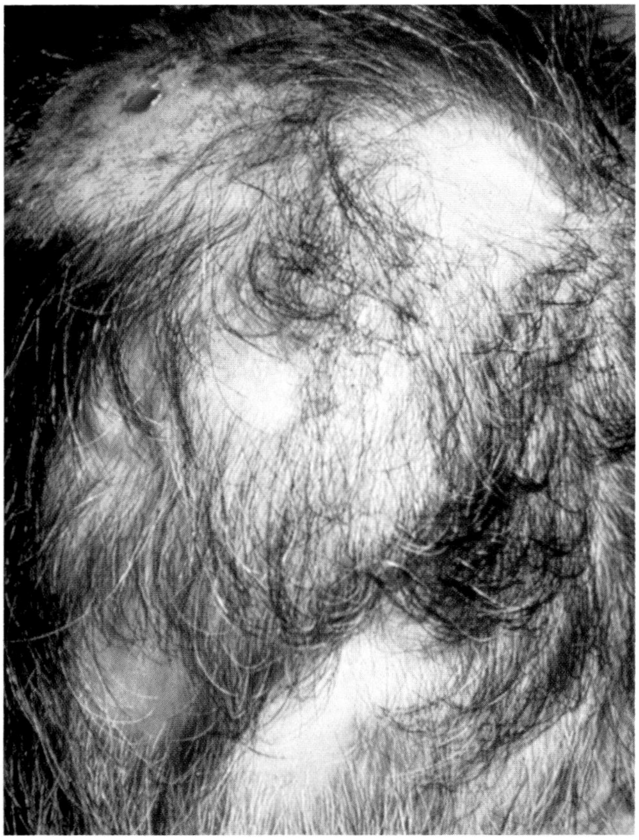

Figure 90. Pseudopelade

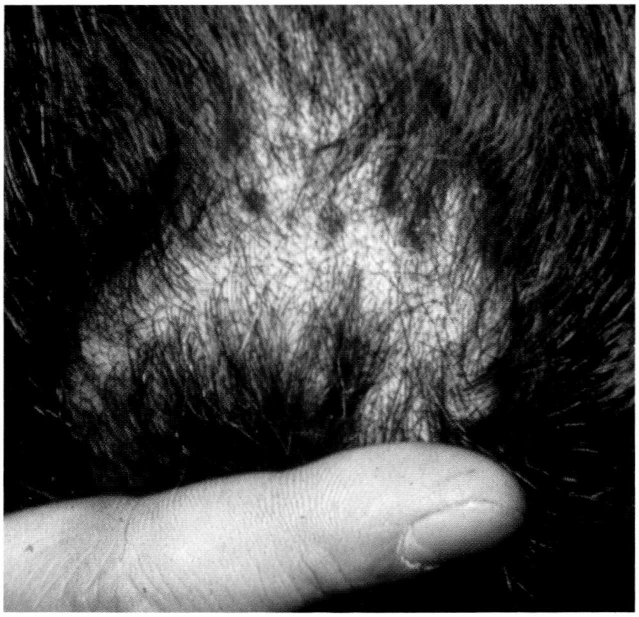

Figure 91. Trichotillomania

Figure 92. Folliculitis decalvans

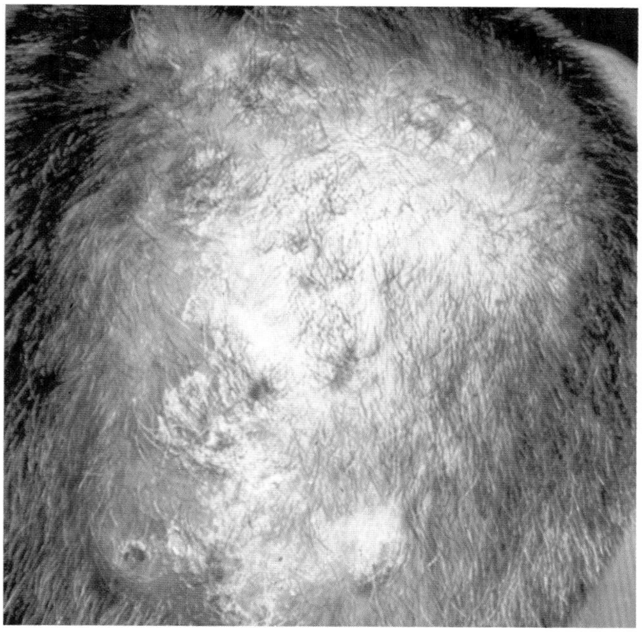

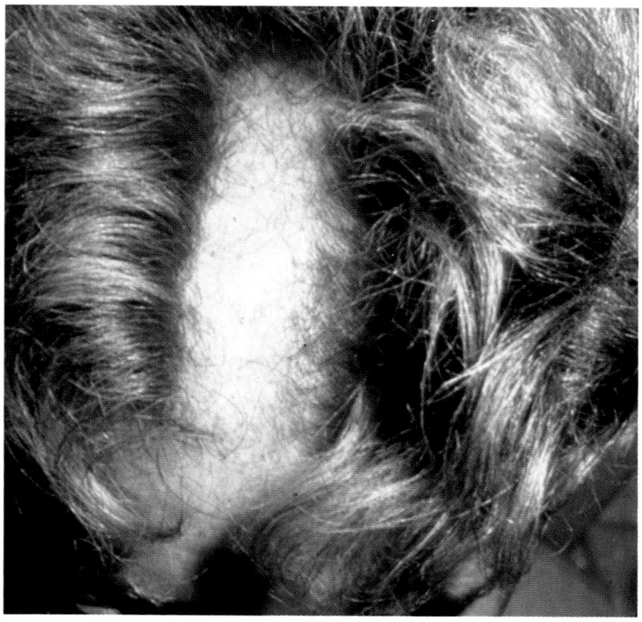

Figure 93. Linear scleroderma

CICATRICIAL ALOPECIAS

The scars following exposure to potent physical agents such as x-ray or heat are usually self-evident, and alopecia is only incidental. Hair loss due to infections is recognizable by the inflammatory reaction. *Tinea capitis* (kerion type) presents an exudative red inflammation which may leave a bald, scarred area. The inflammatory reaction of *favus* may be less intense but more extensive. Folliculitis due to bacterial agents may occasionally destroy the hair bulb, but in *folliculitis decalvans* no specific organisms have been isolated consistently. The end result of folliculitis decalvans may be a scarring, irregular alopecia simulating the end stages of *pseudopelade*. Dissecting cellulitis of the scalp occurs as a persistent, boggy, purulent series of intercommunicating abscesses in the scalp. It is thought to be due to an inflammatory reaction of the scalp apocrine glands analogous to hidradenitis suppurativa in the axilla. Severe viral infections such as *herpes zoster* may leave scarred areas of the scalp, with permanent hair loss.

Nodular lesions with alopecia may occur in leprosy, tuberculosis, tertiary syphilis, sarcoidosis, and the deep mycotic infections. The specific diagnosis must be made, usually by laboratory procedures–biopsy, cultures, or examinations of the direct smear. Neoplastic lesions–primary or metastatic–may be associated with hair loss of the localized type.

Atropic lesions with alopecia occur in discoid lupus erythematosus, lichen planus, morphea, and pseudopelade. In *discoid lupus erythematosus*, the morphology of an atrophic scarred center with a scaling border and follicular plugging usually makes the nature of the alopecia evident. Similarly, the presence of the morphologic features of *lichen planus* and *morphea* usually distinguishes these alopecias. Occasionally, however, the healed end stages of these diseases may leave only white, firm, atrophic cicatricial plaques resembling the "footprints in the snow" pattern of pseudopelade.

Diseases of the Mouth

The diagnosis of diseases of the oral mucosa is somewhat more difficult than that of diseases of the skin. Although many inflammatory lesions of the skin and oral mucosa are essentially the same, their clinical appearance is often quite different. Oral mucous membranes lack a stratum corneum and are bathed with secretions; hence, their surfaces are moist rather than dry like the skin. The horny layer of the oral mucosa is macerated by saliva, which causes vesicular or bullous lesions to rupture easily. Lesions of the mouth may be helpful in the diagnosis of skin diseases although the opposite is more apt to be the case. Mouth lesions that are of diagnostic aid in systemic disease are Koplik spots in measles, the strawberry tongue in scarlatina, the bald tongue in pellagra, glossitis in pernicious anemia, pustules in variola, mucous patches in syphilis, ulcerations in agranulocytic angina, and hemorrhages in scurvy and purpura hemorrhagica.

It is convenient to divide these diseases of the mouth into the following categories:

Local
Systemic
Dermatological
Tongue involvement
Allergic

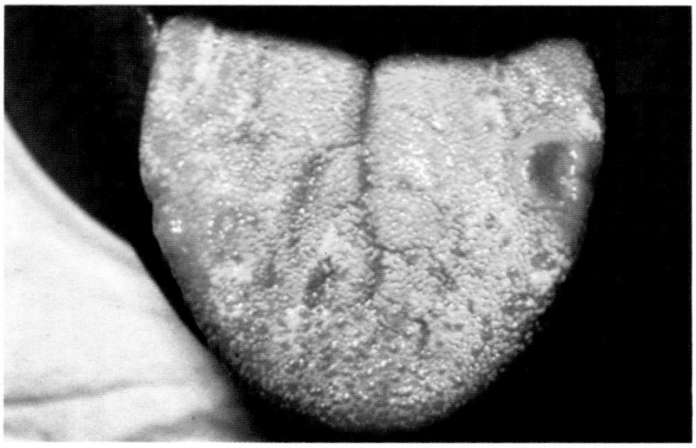

Figure 94. Aphthosis

LOCAL

1. Simple catarrhal stomatitis may be acute or chronic; inciting causes are chemicals, glass blowers, alcohol, tobacco, mouth washes, drugs, thermal conditions, toxic agents (excretion of mercury, bismuth, iodine), infective monilia, perlèche, and electrogalvanic burns.
2. Ulcerogingival stomatitis can be a further exaggeration of simple catarrhal stomatitis, usually caused by ingestion of heavy metals.
3. Acute ulceromembranous stomatitis (Vincent disease).
4. Maculofibrinous stomatitis (aphthae) is usually due to gastrointestinal disturbances or allergy (oatmeal, tomato, nuts, pickles, etc).
5. Periadenitis mucosa necrotica recurrens (Sutton).
6. Leukoplakia is a disease of the greatest importance because of its relationship to cancer. The sites of predilection are the dorsum of the tongue, the cheeks, and the commissurae of the lips, although sometimes the palate is affected. Although the essential cause is unknown, there are many factors that at least contribute to its causation. The disease usually occurs in adult life of the fifth decade or later and is much more common in men than in women. The inciting cause of leukoplakia is usually some form of local irritation, especially tobacco smoke, the disease often being referred to as "smoker's patches." The irritating effect of decayed, rough, and jagged teeth also is a factor. The appearance of leukoplakia varies according to its duration and development. Initially, it consists of streaks of smooth, rather superficial, grayish-white spots. Later the patches become thickened, rough, and stiff with no subjective symptoms until fissures or ulcers appear.
7. Congenital anomalies
   a. Torus palatini
   b. Fordyce disease—This affliction is caused by ectopic sebaceous glands. It is present in 70% of the total population and consists of yellowish

or yellowish-white pinhead maculopapules occurring on the mucous membranes of the lips and cheeks. This condition rarely produces subjective symptoms.

8. Tumors
   a. The tumors most frequently seen include the benign cyst, ranula, fibroma, epulis, papilloma, and angioma. Granuloma pyogenicum is an essentially harmless though often annoying lesion occurring on any part of the body, presumably after some break in the continuity of the skin. It is commonly observed on the lips and occasionally on the tongue. The small tumors consist of extremely vascular granulation tissue which bleeds profusely on slight trauma. The tumors, round or oval, vary in size from a pea to a cherry and are reddish or purplish in color. They are easily removed with the actual cautery, but unless the base is thoroughly cauterized, there is a marked tendency for recurrence.
   b. Malignant tumor (squamous cell epithelioma).

SYSTEMIC

1. Syphilis
   a. Primary–3%-5% of the lesions are extragenital.
   b. Secondary–Papular syphilid of Fournier and mucous patches.
   c. Gumma
2. Tuberculosis
   a. Lupus vulgaris
   b. Tuberculous chancre
   c. Tuberculous orificialis (ulcerosa)–This may appear as a simple ulcer of a nodular, fissured type and may be papillomatous or vegetating.

Tuberculosis of the oral cavity is usually secondary to tuberculosis of the lungs or larynx or is due to extension by continuity of lupus vulgaris of the nose. Primary tuberculosis of the tongue is rare. Tuberculous ulcers of the mouth occur on the tongue, cheeks, and lips and may be single or multiple, soft, rather superficial, bleed easily, are usually painful, and show no tendency to heal. Syphilis and carcinoma are differentiated by diagnosing the bacilli in smears or by animal inoculations. Lupus vulgaris primarily affects the skin. In the majority of cases the disease invades the nose and mouth. In the mouth it appears as papillomatous plaques on the cheeks, gums, and palate.

3. Deficiency diseases
   a. Pellagra and ariboflavinosis
   b. Plummer-Vinson syndrome
   c. Scurvy and sprue
4. Blood dyscrasias
   a. Purpura hemorrhagica of both skin and mucous membranes is easily recognized by the fact that the color does not disappear upon pressure and even remains after death. The blood platelets are reduced and the bleeding time is increased. The clot fails to retract and expressed serum is normal.
   b. Leukemias
   c. Osler disease
   d. Polycythemia vera
5. Leishmaniasis

   This is a tropical disease usually beginning on the skin as one or more indolent ulcers, which may per-

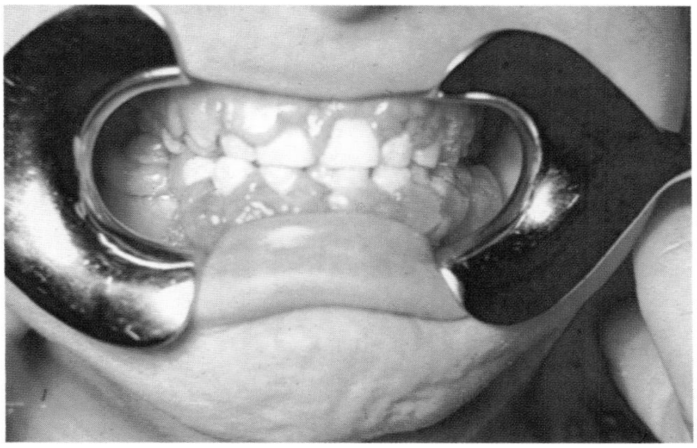

Figure 95. Leukemia of the gums

sist for years. In 15%-20% of the cases, leishmaniasis eventually attacks the nasal mucosa and may extend to the pharynx, with the production of severe deformities.

6. Pigmentary diseases
   a. Addison disease
   b. Acanthosis nigricans
7. Metabolic, hormonal, and contagious diseases
8. Triple-symptom complex

DERMATOLOGICAL

1. Lichen planus

   Lichen planus produces lesions of the mouth in about one third of the cases. Lichen planus of the mouth may precede the cutaneous eruption, probably more often than is supposed. It is usually unnoticed until the appearance of skin lesions, since involvement of the mouth rarely produces subjective symptoms and the condition habitually disappears without local treatment. The mouth lesions appear as tiny grayish dots, streaks, and circles, and a combination of these forms produces a reticulated appearance. Ordinarily, there is little or no appreciable infiltration and never any ulceration. The diagnosis becomes difficult only when the lesions coalesce and form a diffuse area on the dorsum of the tongue. The eruption occurs most often on the mucosa of the cheeks, opposite the molars, and along the interdental clefts. The dorsum of the tongue is the second-most frequent site of involvement. Lichen planus may be confined to the mouth for months or years without any outbreak of cutaneous lesions. The chief point of medical interest in lichen planus of the mouth is the differential diagnosis from leukoplakia.

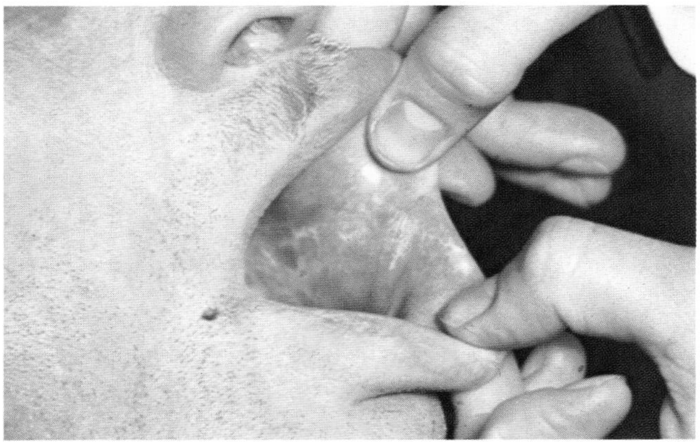

Figure 96. Lichen planus

2. Pemphigus vulgaris

   This is the most important of the diseases in which vesicles and bullae appear in the mouth. It is rare to see uninterrupted bullae in the mouth, as the lesions are broken soon after their formation, through maceration. The mouth lesions of pemphigus are of special interest, as they may precede cutaneous eruption by months or even years. All parts of the mouth may be affected, and the lesions appear as raw, painful, red patches partly covered by shreds of epidermis. In some patients the organisms of Vincent angina are abundant, but they merely represent a secondary infection. When there are numerous lesions of the mouth, they may cause not only marked pain and suffering but may also interfere with proper nutrition.
3. Erythema multiforme bullosum (Stevens-Johnson syndrome)

   These lesions are frequently observed following foreign protein injections, ingestion of certain foods and drugs, or with infectious processes.
4. Drug eruptions

   Dermatitis medicamentosa (stomatitis medicamentosa); coal tar derivatives, iodides, and bromides are frequently reported as causative agents.
5. Secondary syphilis
6. Vincent infection
7. Impetigo
8. Herpes simplex

   This condition may involve the buccal mucous

membranes as an extension from the vermillion border of the lips. It is an uncommon affliction unless aphthous ulcers are considered to be a form of intraoral herpes.

9. Herpes zoster
   Herpes zoster is rarely encountered in the mouth and occurs only with involvement of the second division of the fifth nerve. In the above condition, the disease affects only one side of the tongue, the mucous surface of the cheeks, palate, tonsil, and perhaps the pharynx and larynx.
10. Lupus erythematosus
    This disease of the mouth frequently affects the cheek pouches close to the molars. It is normally well defined, with bluish or red raised borders and a slightly depressed, eroded center. Later the center may present grayish or whitish points or streaks. The most striking feature is the sharply delimitated border and irregular shape. When there is involvement of the vermillion border, it is an aid to the proper diagnosis.
11. Urticaria and angioneurotic edema may affect the mucous membranes of the mouth. Angioneurotic edema is a circumscribed swelling that commonly attains its maximum size in a few minutes or, infrequently, in an hour and then disappears in one or two days. Angioneurotic edema may occur on any part of the body but is seen most frequently about the lips, although the tongue may be affected and, even more important, the glottis.
12. Moniliasis
13. Fordyce disease

TONGUE INVOLVEMENT

1. Acute phase
   a. Caused by infection
   b. Caused by mechanical interference
2. Chronic phase
   a. Brought about by dietary deficiency

Figure 97. (top) Tuberculosis of the tongue

Figure 98. (middle) Vitamin "B" deficiency

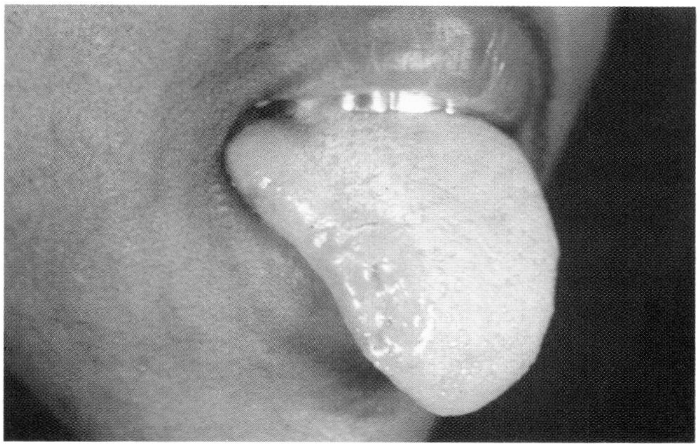

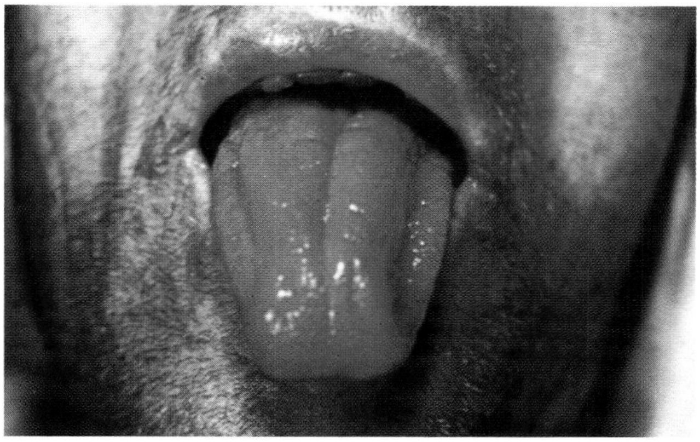

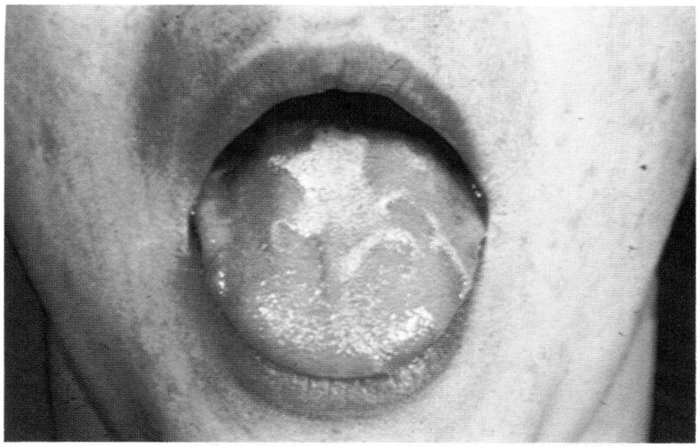

Figure 99. Geographic tongue

b. Brought about by blood dyscrasias
c. Results from metabolic diseases

3. Discolorations
 a. A coated tongue may result from a diet of milk, hypochlorhydria, mouth breathing, alkaline diet, or infection. The ordinary treatment is scrubbing the area with a brush and soap and water.
 b. Black hairy tongue, *lingua nigra*, consists of fur-like patches that are blackish-brown or yellowish-brown and situated on the dorsum of the tongue anterior to the circumvallate papillae. The disease is a hyperkeratosis of the filiform papillae, doubtless caused by some irritation, the deposit of pigment being secondary and resulting from external causes. The black color is due to iron compounds from the decomposition of hemoglobin that is deposited on the dead keratinized epithelium of the papillae. Ordinarily, the disease causes no subjective symptoms and the patient may be unaware of its existence. In mild cases, prompt relief is obtained by swabbing the tongue with hydrogen peroxide followed by an application of warm, physiologic salt solution.
4. Inflammation
 a. Simple glossitis
 b. Chemical irritation
 c. Heat
5. Secondary glossitis
 a. Measles, scarlet fever, varicella
 b. Moeller glossitis, usually associated with pernicious anemia
 c. Glossodynia, usually associated with anemias
 d. Leukoplakia
 e. Erythema migrans, *lingua geographica* (also known as wandering rash, transitory benign plaques of the tongue), is a rather uncommon disease occurring in children as well as adults. It is a superficial inflammatory disease occurring on the dorsum

Figure 100. (top) Black hairy tongue

Figure 101. (middle) Scarlet fever

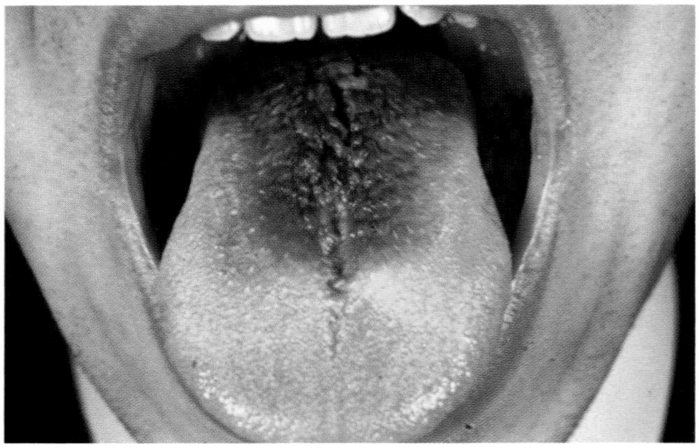

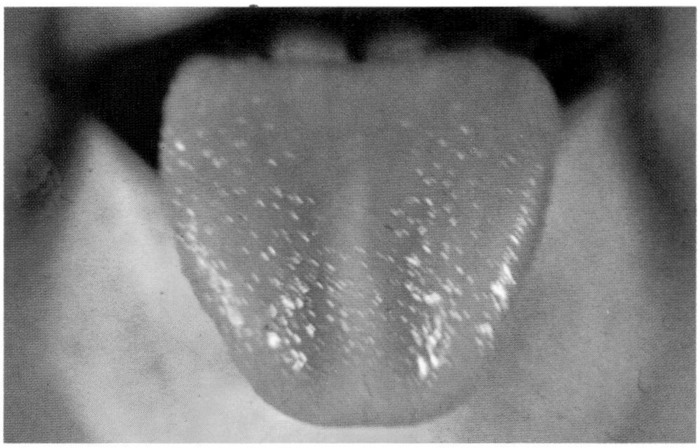

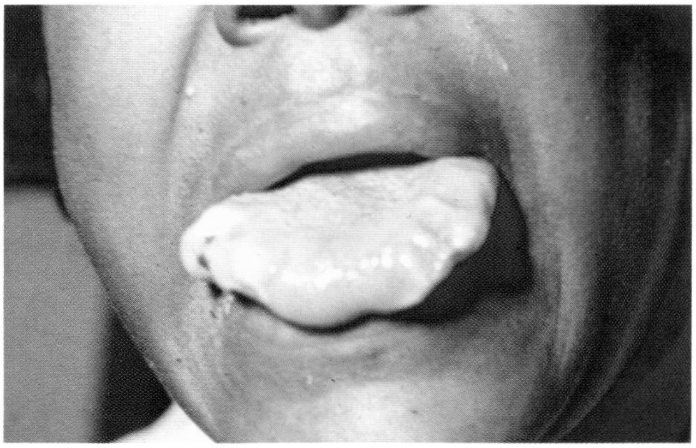

Figure 102. Amyloidosis

Figure 103. Lymphangioma

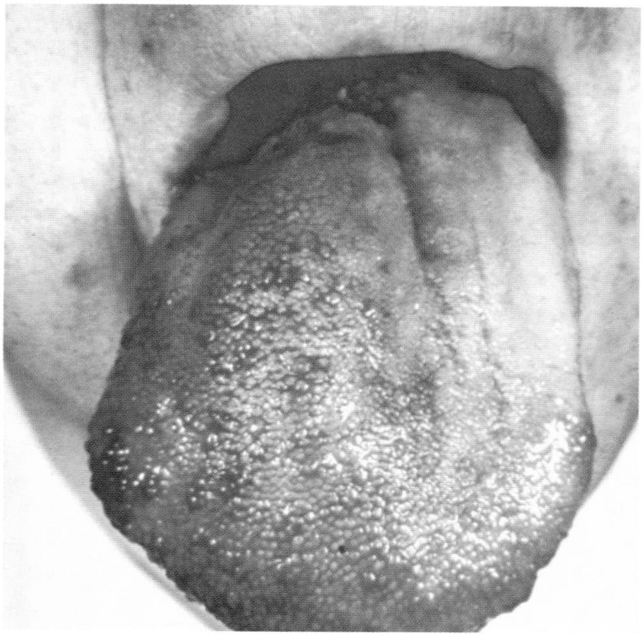

tip and sides of the tongue as one or a cluster of pea-sized patches which tend to enlarge centrifugally and frequently coalesce. The latter causes a polycyclic or map-like appearance. The patches are slightly elevated and appear red in the center with a whitish or yellowish border. An individual lesion runs its course within a week or less, but because of the constant formation of new patches the process may continue for years. Subjective symptoms are almost always absent.

  f. Median rhombodial glossitis – a congenital anomaly

6. Tumors
   a. Benign (granuloma pyogenicum)
   b. Malignant
7. Congenital

Scrotal tongue, sometimes called grooved tongue, refers to the furrows and ridges of varying depth due either to some preceding glossitis or to an inherited

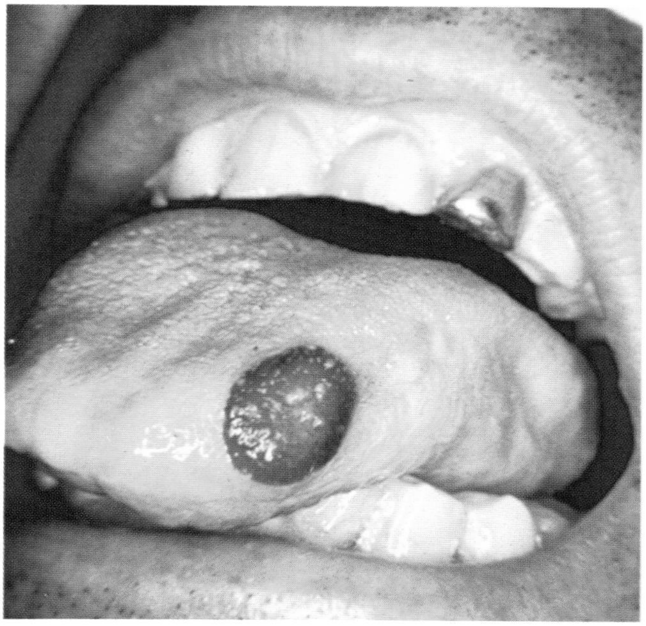

Figure 104. Squamous carcinoma

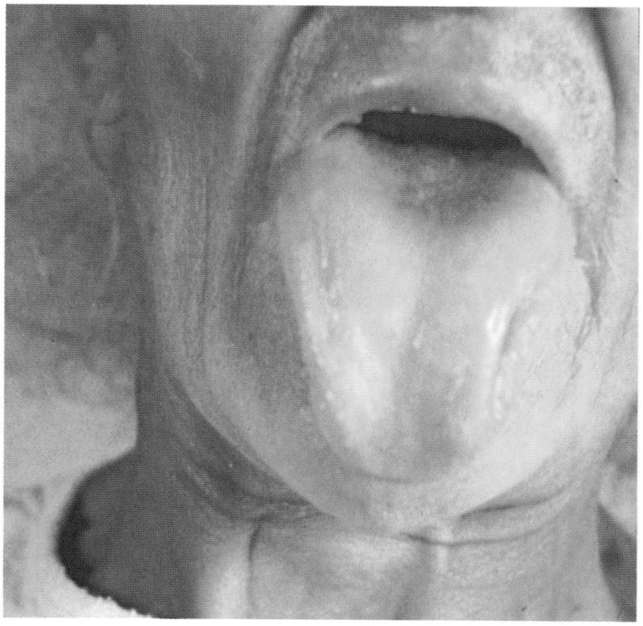

Figure 105. Iron-deficiency glossitis

familial trait. The furrows are both longitudinal and transverse, and the tongue is apt to be slightly enlarged. The scrotal tongue is red and free from coating and rarely causes subjective symptoms.

ALLERGIC

1. Erythematous or purpuric mucous membranes of the mouth associated with burning and edema resulting from wheat, eggs, tomatoes, chocolate, or milk.
2. Aphthae stomatitis
3. Contact stomatitis and cheilitis caused by lipstick, mouthwash, tobacco, cigarette paper, or toothpaste.

Lesions of the Genitalia

The diseases of the genitalia are modified by moisture and the proximity of body folds. Common bullous diseases rapidly become erosive, whereas scaly diseases, such as psoriasis, lose their scales, and intertriginous lesions may spread to the genitalia.

In the differential diagnosis of any genital lesion, primary syphilis should be first considered until specifically ruled out.

SYPHILITIC CHANCRE

Chancres generally occur as single lesions, but multiple lesions are not rare. The lesion is usually an eroded papule that is decidedly firm and indurated while the surface may be crusted or ulcerated. The chancre is typically painless, but a dark-field examination will disclose *Treponema pallidum.*

CHANCROID LESIONS

The lesions appear as multiple, soft, tender erosions or ulcerations with a grayish base. Both the lesions and the associated lymphadenopathy, often more pronounced on one side, are quite painful. Dark-field examination is negative. *H. ducreyi,* the causative organism, may be extracted from the lesion by a direct stained smear or by culture.

GRANULOMA INGUINALE

This disease is characterized by a soft, painless, raised, raw-beef colored, smooth, granulating lesion. There is no significant lymphadenopathy, the dark-field is negative, and the serologic tests are nonreactive. The pathognomonic *Donovan bodies (Donovania granulomatis)* are best demonstrated by direct tissue-spread smears stained with hematological dyes, i.e., Giemsa or Wright stain. Biopsy may demonstrate the causative organism.

LYMPHOGRANULOMA VENEREUM

The initial lesion is a small, transient, rarely seen vesicoulcer. The patient shows unilateral, painful, inguinal

Figure 106. (top) Chancre
Figure 107. (middle) Chancroid

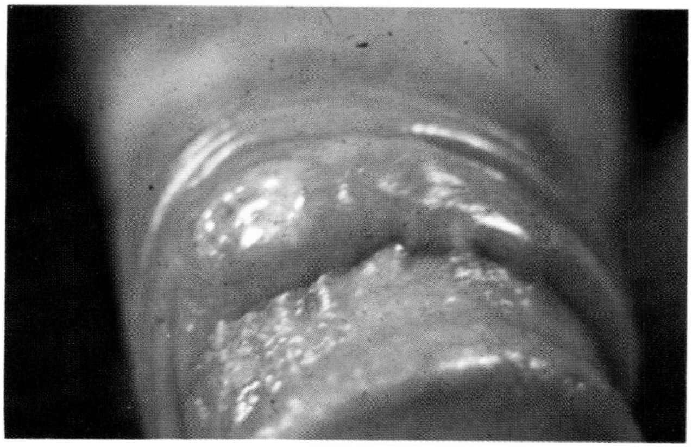

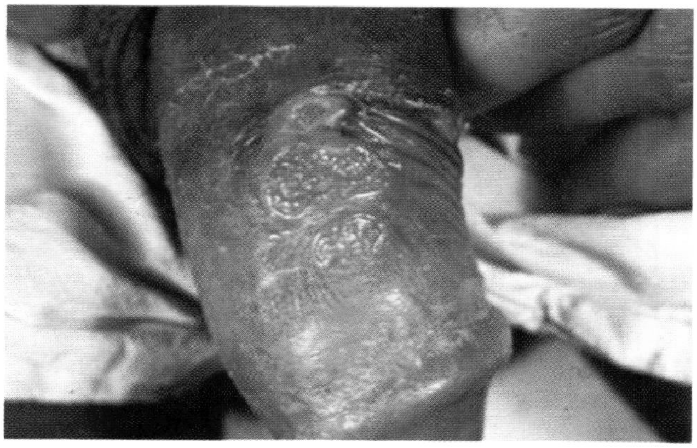

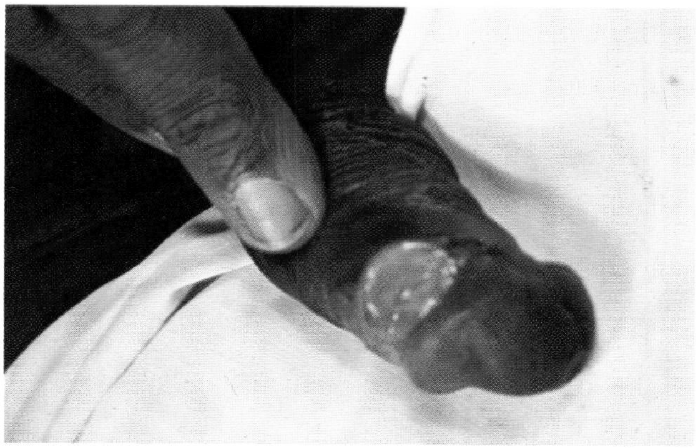

Figure 108. Granuloma inguinale

Figure 109. Herpes progenitalis

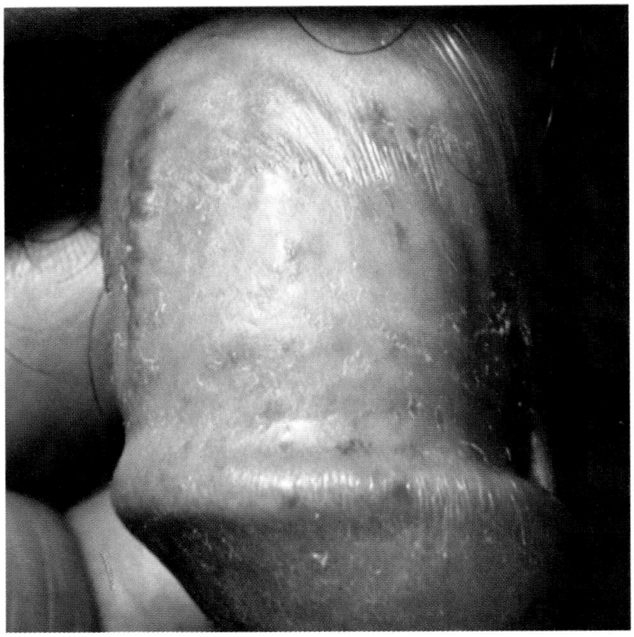

lymphadenopathy. A rising titer, detected by complement fixation tests against the causative organism *Bedsonia lymphogranulomatosis* is diagnostic. The Frei skin test is positive.

HERPES PROGENITALIS

This viral disease is manifested by grouped, painful, vesicular lesions. A case history usually reveals recurrent lesions at the same site. The smear technique demonstrates typical viral "balloon" cells.

CARCINOMA

Often the lesion has been present for a considerable

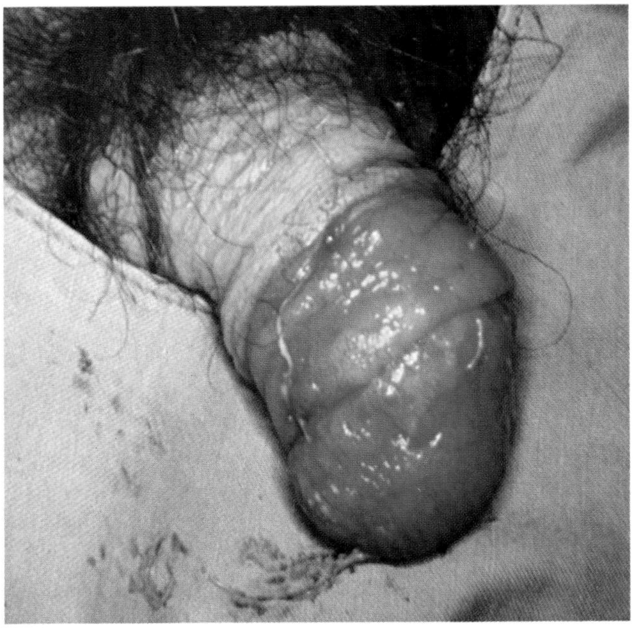

Figure 110. Squamous cell carcinoma

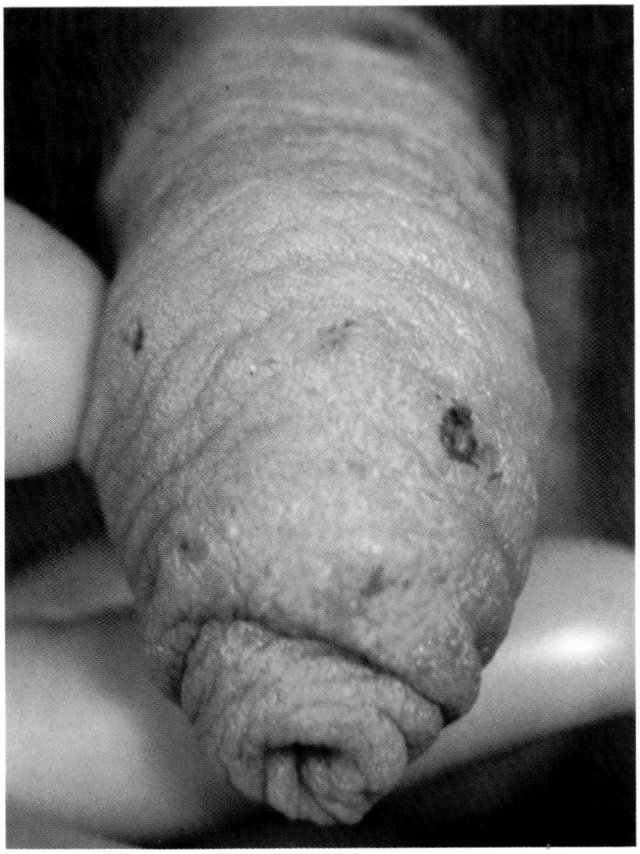

Figure 111. Scabies

period of time. The diagnosis is established by biopsy of any suspicious fungating or infiltrating ulcerative lesion.

SCABIES

Pruritic vesicles with burrow formation are highly suggestive. Finding of the mite in the burrow is diagnostic.

BALANITIS

A history of trauma is usual. The dark-field and serologic tests are negative.

LICHEN PLANUS

Genital lesions are usually annular or typical polygonal, flat-topped, violaceous papules. They may be pruritic and either single or multiple.

PSORIASIS

This disease often presents an erythematous or erythemato-squamous plaque on the glans. Removal of the scale produces pinpoint bleeding.

DRUG ERUPTIONS

One site of predilection of a "fixed" *dermatitis medicamentosa* is the genital region. Antipyrine, phenolphthalein, phenacetin, barbiturates, salicylates, sulfonamides, and antibiotics are reported to be the most-common inciting agents. Careful inquiry should be made as to drug ingestion.

REITER SYNDROME

Lesions on genitalia resemble psoriasis. Reiter syndrome is frequently associated with urethritis, conjunctivis, and arthritis.

PEMPHIGUS

Pemphigus vulgaris and *pemphigus vegetans* may involve the genitalia and are demonstrated by the appearance of bullous lesions.

PELLAGRA

Erythematous lesions on the genitalia may be associated with *pellagra*.

FUNGUS INFECTIONS

Superficial yeast infections *(moniliasis)*, as well as deep infections such as *histoplasmosis*, may occur on the genitalia.

PSEUDOXANTHOMA ELASTICUM

This is an inherited disorder that affects the elastic tissue. In addition to the skin, it may affect the eyes and the

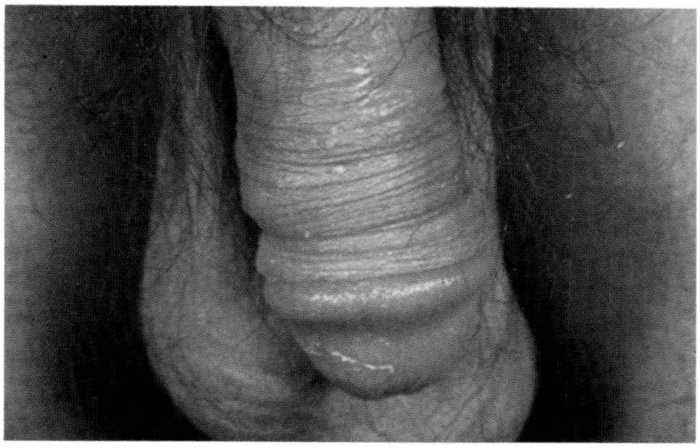

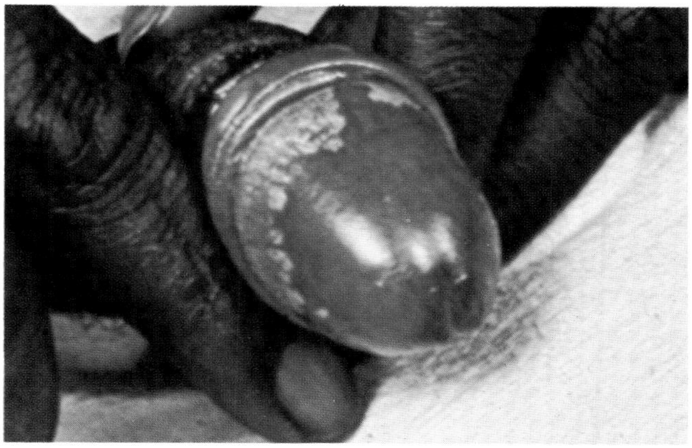

Figure 112. (top) Psoriasis
Figure 113. (bottom) Pellagra

cardiovascular system. The lesions are small, yellowish-brown papules that tend to be aggregated in groups and are parallel to the skin folds.

LICHEN SCLEROSUS ET ATROPHICUS

White atrophic patches surrounded by an erythematous halo are characteristic of this disorder. This disease is most common in women; the male counterpart is *balanitis xerotica obliterans.*

CONDYLOMA ACUMINATUM (venereal warts)

These lesions affect the mucocutaneous surfaces and form extensive vegetating masses.

LEUKEMIA

Leukemic nodules, as well as nodules of Kaposi sarcoma, may occur on the genitalia.

Tumors of the Skin

The skin is not a homogeneous organ and consists of a diversity of components from both ectodermal and mesodermal origins. Each of these components may give rise to its own group of tumors. Over 100 different types of skin tumors have been described in the literature.

Tumors may arise from the surface epidermis or from the epidermal appendages such as hair follicles, sebaceous glands, and sweat glands. Others are derived from melanocytes, the pigment-producing cells, and some arise from the various components of the dermis, such as connective tissue cells, blood vessels, and cutaneous lymphoreticular cells. Another group of tumors originate elsewhere and spread to the skin by direct extension or by metastasis.

It is obvious from the diversity of origin of skin tumors as well as from their variable significance that an accurate diagnosis is essential before undertaking therapy. Radical surgery for a misdiagnosed benign tumor is as indefensible as inadequate excision of a highly malignant tumor. Both errors are avoidable by obtaining a biopsy and an accurate pathologic diagnosis. With small lesions, an excisional biopsy will both remove the lesion and provide diagnostic material. Biopsy of the larger lesions at one or more representative areas for diagnostic examination is often indicated. There is no evidence that such an incisional biopsy will disseminate viable tumor cells; the pathologic diagnosis will enable the clinician to plan his therapy more intelligently.

TUMORS OF THE SURFACE EPIDERMIS

Important tumors of the surface epidermis include verruca, seborrheic keratosis, actinic keratosis, Bowen disease, and squamous cell carcinoma.

Verruca vulgaris (common wart) is a common tumor of childhood and young adult life. In contrast to other tumors, verrucae are known to be caused by a virus that invades epidermal cells and stimulates a typical proliferation.

Figure 114. Warts

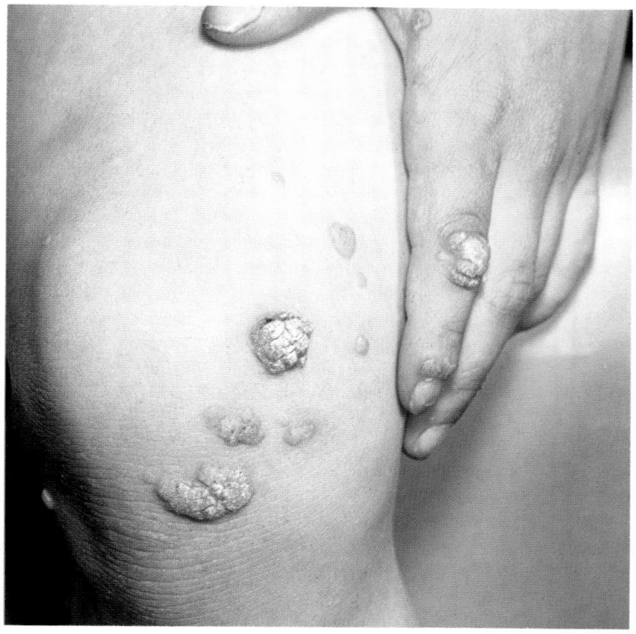

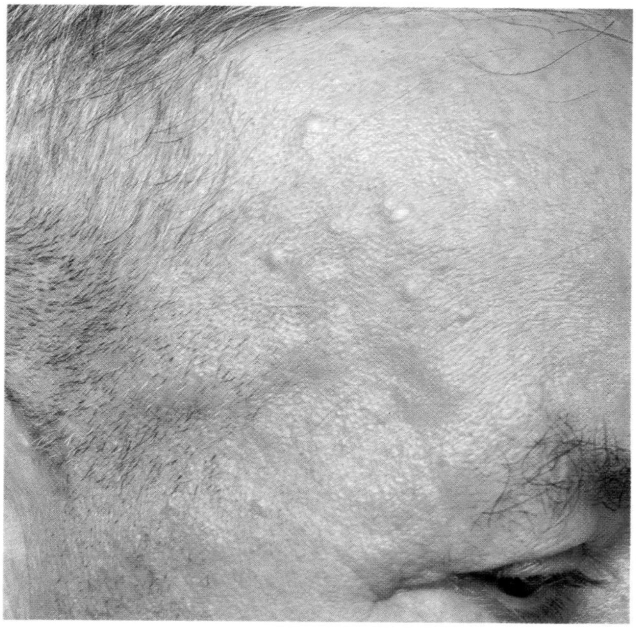

Figure 115. Epithelial cysts

Figure 116. Seborrheic keratoses

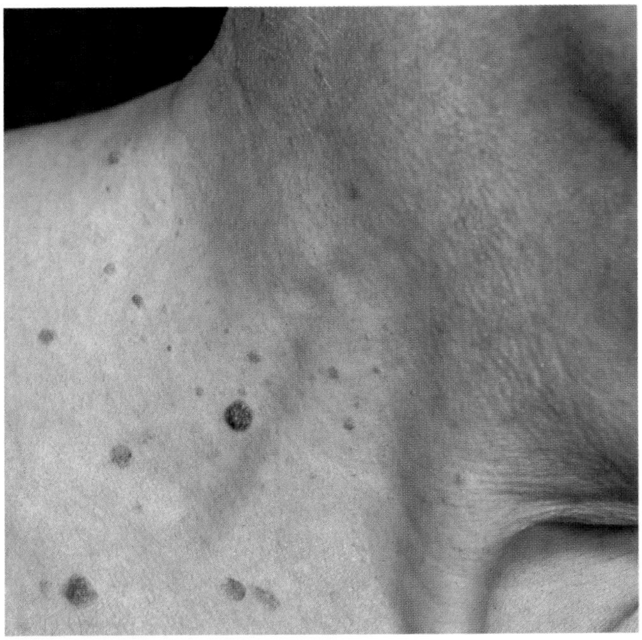

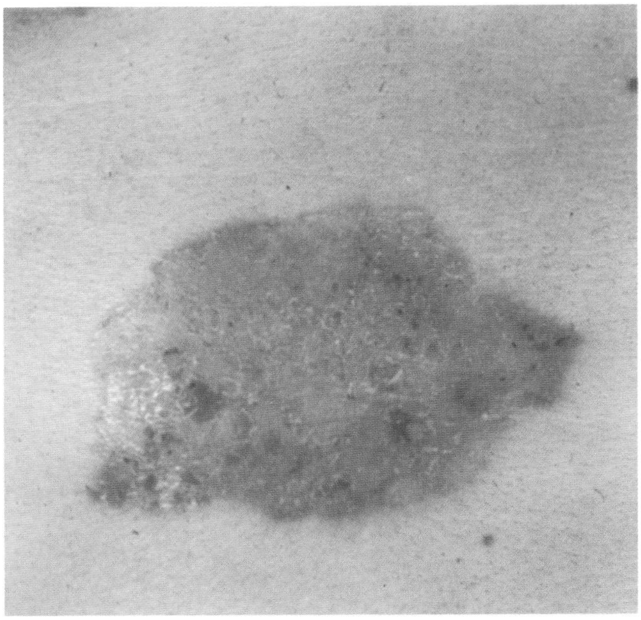

Figure 117. Superficial epithelioma

The lesions occur anywhere on the skin surface but are particularly common on the extremities. The most-common form appears as a variably sized, elevated, sessile lesion with a rough keratotic surface. *Verrucae* may be single or multiple, and multiple lesions frequently are preceded by a solitary lesion of variable duration. Other forms of *verrucae* include juvenile flat warts, plantar warts, and condyloma acuminata.

The recommended forms of treatment include electrosurgical or chemical destruction, cryotherapy with solid carbon dioxide or liquid nitrogen, and surgical excision.

Seborrheic keratoses (basal cell papillomas) are one of the most common of all cutaneous tumors, which usually occur as multiple papules on the face, trunk, and arms of older people. They are often deeply pigmented, elevated, round to oval papules which give the distinct impression of being stuck onto the skin surface rather than occurring within it. The surface is markedly irregular with small keratin-filled crypts and frequently with a thin greasy scale.

Seborrheic keratosis is a benign lesion and is usually easily diagnosed. It should not be confused with malignant melanoma, which also is deeply pigmented. Surface removal of seborrheic keratosis results in complete cure without scar formation. Surgical excision is not necessary.

Actinic keratoses (senile keratoses) occur on older individuals and are limited to sun-exposed areas such as the face, and dorsa of the hands. They present one or more light-brown erythematous flat lesions which are less elevated than seborrheic keratoses and are more adherent to the skin. The surface is often irregular with a firmly adherent keratotic consistency. Actinic keratosis is a premalignant lesion, and approximately 25% of untreated cases will progress to frank squamous cell carcinoma after a number of years.

Local removal with a dermal curette and cautery or

electrodesiccation of the base constitutes the usual treatment of uncomplicated actinic keratoses.

Bowen disease is another premalignant epidermal lesion frequently appearing as an irregular erythematous plaque, the border of which is sharply defined and frequently slightly elevated. The most-common location is the trunk, although lesions may occur anywhere on the cutaneous surface. Multiple lesions are less common than is a single one.

Malignant transformation of Bowen disease is uncommon but can result in an invasive squamous cell carcinoma. Of greater significance than the lesion of Bowen disease is the statistically significant association of Bowen disease with carcinoma elsewhere. The associated carcinoma is usually detected on an average of 5 to 7 years following the onset of the skin lesion. Common sites for the associated carcinoma are the skin, respiratory tract, gastrointestinal tract, and genitourinary system. The treatment of Bowen disease includes surgical excision or electrosurgical destruction.

Squamous cell carcinoma of the skin appears most frequently on exposed surfaces of older individuals. It may arise as a preexisting lesion such as actinic keratosis or may arise *de novo* from sun-damaged skin. The most-frequent locations are the lower lip, face, external ear, and dorsum of the hand. The lesion develops as a slowly enlarging nodule with a keratotic surface. Usually a central ulcer develops surrounded by a wide, rolled border. Although regional lymph node metastases are common from squamous cell carcinoma of the lip, they are considerably less frequent with lesions arising on hair-bearing skin.

Treatment will depend upon the extent and location of the lesion but will usually consist of surgery, electrosurgery, irradiation, or chemosurgery.

TUMORS OF THE EPIDERMAL APPENDAGES

A large variety of tumors arise from epithelial cells of

Figure 118. Squamous cell carcinoma

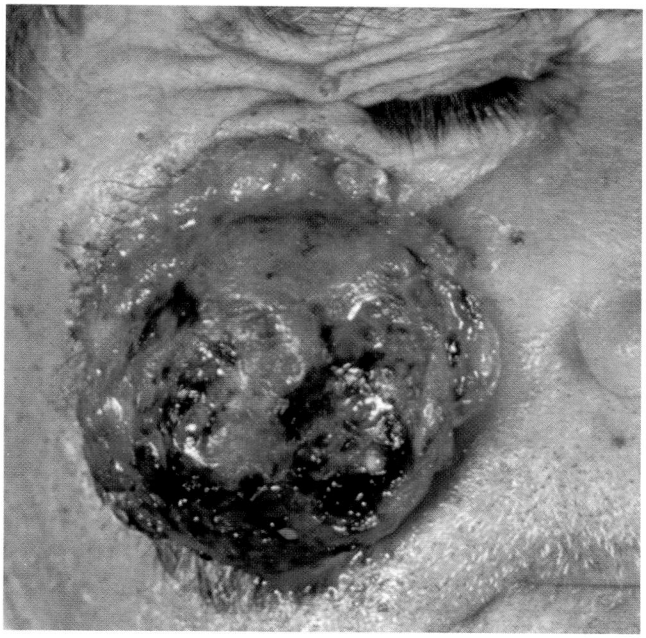

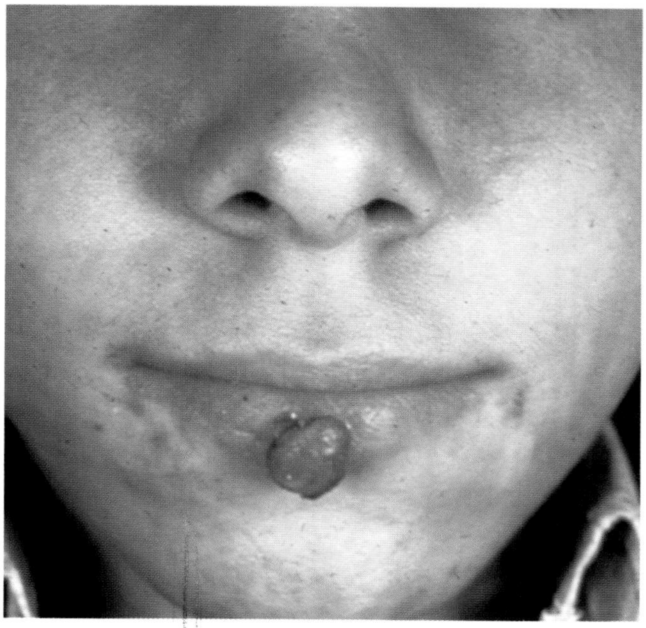

Figure 119. Granuloma pyogenicum

the epidermal appendages with differentiation toward sweat glands, sebaceous glands, and pilar structures. Most are benign and carry the designation of adenoma.

The most-common tumor of this origin, however, is malignant and represents the common malignant skin tumor, basal cell carcinoma. These tumors are believed to arise from immature pluripotential cells of the epidermis, with capacity to form epidermal appendages.

Basal cell carcinomas usually occur on the face and neck of adults, and chronic exposure to sunlight is an important associated factor. Several types of clinical lesions may occur; the most common is the nodular type, which appears as a smooth, somewhat translucent nodule with a few telangiectatic vessels across the surface. As the lesion enlarges, the center becomes depressed and ultimately ulcerates with the formation of a peripheral, rolled border. At this stage, the lesion is frequently termed *rodent ulcer.* Without treatment, basal cell carcinoma will grow relentlessly and cause ever-enlarging areas of tissue destruction. In spite of the locally invasive nature of this tumor, metastases are most uncommon. This behavior pattern differentiates basal cell carcinoma from other malignant tumors.

Other clinical types of basal cell carcinoma include plaque-like lesions resembling Bowen disease, deeply pigmented nodules, and sclerotic indurated lesions.

The treatment of basal cell carcinoma varies, depending upon the site and location of the lesion. The four accepted therapeutic approaches are curettage and electrodesiccation or cautery, surgical excision, irradiation, and chemosurgical destruction.

TUMORS DERIVED FROM MELANOCYTES

The melanocyte, the pigment-producing cell of the skin, originates in the neural crest, and during fetal life migrates into the basal layer of the epidermis where it provides pigment for the basal cells. These melanocytes can give rise to a number of tumors, of which the major-

Figure 120. Basal cell epithelioma

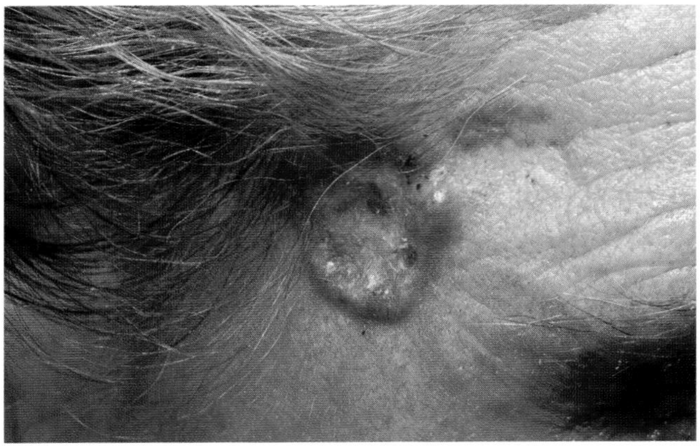

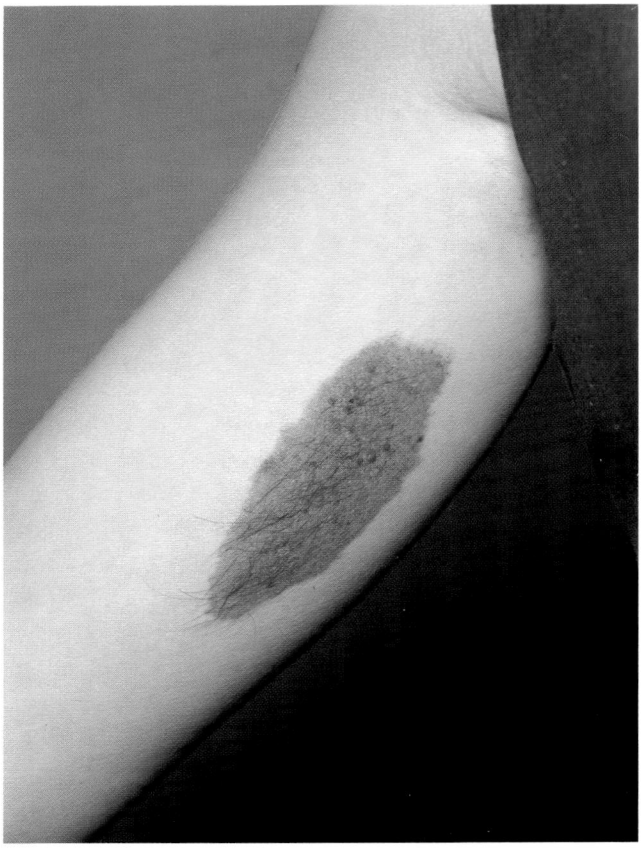

Figure 121. Pigmented hairy nevus

ity are benign. The most-common tumor in this group is the *pigmented nevus*, which is composed of nevus cells which are benign tumor cells derived from melanocytes. Nevi are classified as junctional, intradermal, or compound, depending respectively on whether the nests of nevus cells are at (1) the dermoepidermal junction, (2) within the dermis, or (3) in both locations.

Clinically, the lesions are flat to dome-shaped or polypoid and range in size from a few millimeters to a centimeter or more. The lesion is sharply outlined with a regular configuration. Pigmentation ranges from a slight coloration to nearly black.

The common pigmented intradermal nevus is generally benign, and malignant transformation is an exceptional occurrence. Although the vast majority of junction and compound nevi are also benign, a small number are capable of evolving into malignant melanomas. Such malignancy potential in no way necessitates the prophylactic removal of all junction and compound nevi, as it would be a formidable task in individuals with multiple nevi. Instead, such nevi are carefully watched for signs of change and are promptly excised if such alterations occur. These changes include enlargement of previously quiescent lesions, spread of pigment from the nevus into the surrounding skin, development of irregular pigmentation within the lesion, ulceration, bleeding, and the development of unexplained inflammatory variations. Such lesions should be totally excised, with an adequate margin, and subjected to careful microscopic examination.

Malignant melanoma, as the name indicates, is a malignant tumor derived from melanocytic cells. It is among the most serious of malignant tumors and is capable of early and widespread metastases.

It is likely that the great majority of malignant melanomas arise *de novo* as malignant tumors. Others, however, arise from preexisting nevi, as has been discussed earlier.

Figure 122. Malignant melanoma

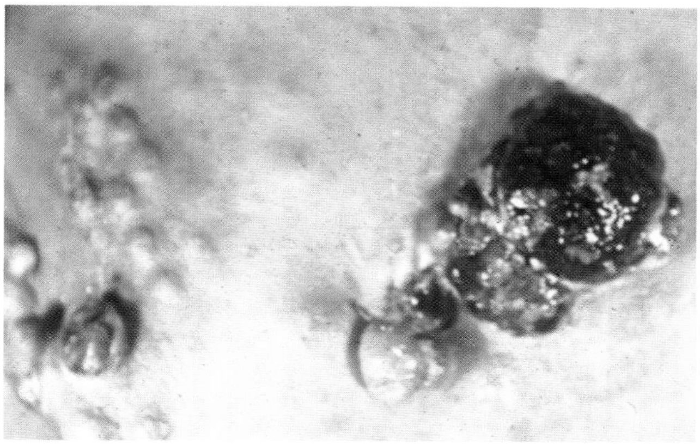

Malignant melanomas vary considerably in appearance. Some resemble ordinary nevi but have irregular pigmentation and irregular borders with pigment spread. Other lesions have a more ominous appearance with ulceration and bleeding. Although most malignant melanomas show some pigmentation, some are nonpigmented.

Malignant melanoma may occur virtually anywhere on the skin surface, but the general predilection is greater on the head, neck, and lower extremities.

The treatment of malignant melanomas consists of total excision, with margins as wide as feasible, as well as appropriate lymph node dissection. Certain advanced cases are treated by palliative chemotherapy or regional profusion.

Benign juvenile melanoma is a lesion that closely resembles malignant melanoma microscopically, but it occurs during childhood. The clinical appearance is nondescript, with the development of a slightly erythematous small nodule in the skin. Less commonly, the lesion is pigmented like an ordinary nevus.

The *blue nevus* clinically resembles an ordinary pigmented nevus but is generally darker. It is composed of heavily pigmented dermal melanocytes rather than nevus cells and is benign.

TUMORS OF MESODERMAL ORIGIN

The various connective tissue cells in the dermis may give rise to tumors, of which the majority are benign. Treatment usually consists of surgical excision.

Fibroblasts and histocytes give rise to the *dermatofibroma*, a benign tumor frequently occurring as an indurated, pigmented nodule on an extremity. *Keloids* represent uncontrolled hyperplasia of dermal connective tissue in response to injury; they are more common in pigmented people, especially blacks, and even though they are not malignant, they are difficult to cure. Keloids are atrophic epithelium and during the early proliferative stage are usually erythematous but they later become pale. They may be distinguished from hypertrophic scars by the fact that they extend well beyond the area of the original injury. Smooth-muscle cells, usually of erector pili muscle origin, give rise to the leiomyoma, a small erythematous, brownish lesion, multiple in occurrence, which may be very painful.

Schwann cells give rise to several dermal tumors, the most frequent of which is the neurofibroma in association with von Recklinghausen disease. Neurofibromas are common, and many individuals have one or two such lesions. More than six or eight neurofibromas accompanied by café-au-lait spots warrant presumptive diagnosis of neurofibromatosis. Neurofibromas may appear as nodules within the skin or as sessile or pedunculated lesions protruding from the surface of the skin. In the latter case, the tumors have usually herniated through the dermis and can be pushed back.

Blood vessels form tumors, and the capillary hemangioma is one of the most common tumors of infancy. It usually is present at birth or appears shortly thereafter as a bright-red spot or a larger vascular area, which may enlarge rapidly during the first few months of life. By six months to one year of age, the lesion has usually reached its maximum extent. Capillary hemangiomas frequently resolve spontaneously and heal with a better cosmetic result than could be achieved by any therapeutic measure.

Other types of hemangiomas include the *cavernous hemangioma*, a deeper lesion composed of more widely dilated vessels and the *nevus flammeus* (port-wine stain). The *nevus flammeus* appears as an irregular, reddish to reddish-blue patch and is composed of dilated, mature capillaries in the upper dermis. The face and neck are the most common locations for *nevus flammeus*, and the process may be associated with other vascular abnormalities (Sturge-Weber syndrome). Malignant tumors of the vascular system do occur in

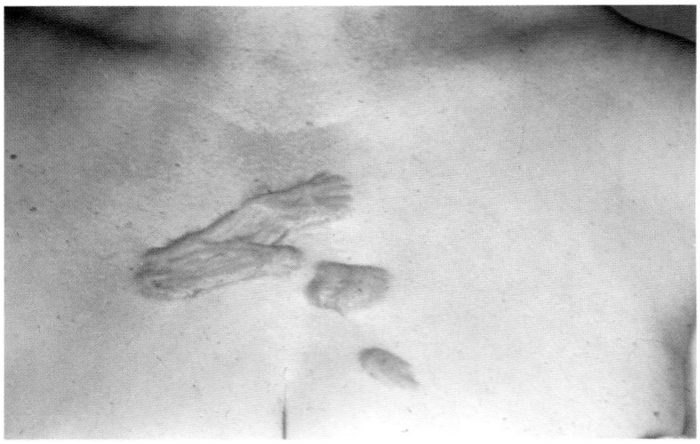

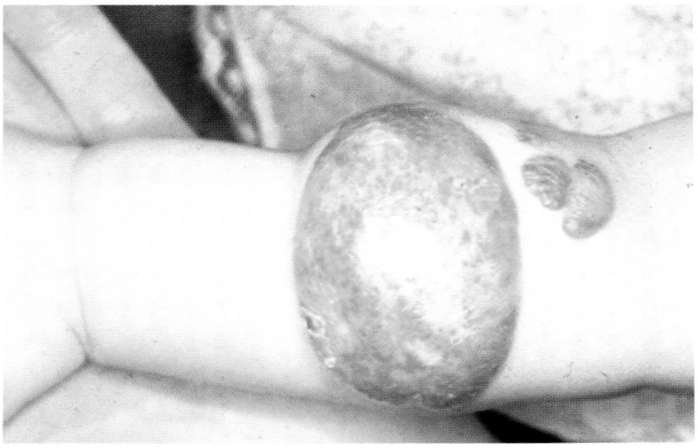

Figure 123. (top) Keloid

Figure 124. (bottom) Strawberry cavernous hemangioma

the skin, and the most common is *Kaposi hemorrhagic sarcoma,* usually seen on the lower legs in men. Malignant hemangioendothelioma rarely occurs in the skin.

Lymphoreticular proliferation: The skin is host to cells of lymphoreticular origin, such as lymphocytes and reticulum cells, both of which can participate in neoplastic processes, benign or malignant. The clinical picture of many lesions will be similar, with differentiation depending upon microscopic examination.

Included in this group are *cutaneous lymphoid hyperplasia,* a benign hyperplasia of preexisting cutaneous lymphoreticular elements, and *lymphocytic and reticulum cell lymphoma,* which is a malignant lymphoreticular proliferation. The lesions usually consist of erythematous to bluish plaques and nodules occurring anywhere on the skin's surface. The malignant lesions have a greater tendency for continuing enlargement and ultimate ulceration. Additionally, skin lesions of malignant lymphoma may have internal involvement.

Treatment of benign lymphoreticular lesions requires excision or superficial irradiation. In lymphoma, the treatment is of the underlying disease.

Mast cell tumors occur primarily in the skin, usually in multiple sites, and are characterized by release of vasodilatory substances, resulting in the formation of wheals when the tumors are injured or exposed to heat. This entity is common in children and is called *urticaria pigmentosa.*

Mycosis fungoides: This lymphoma is limited primarily to the skin with well-demarcated, intensely pruritic plaques resembling psoriasis or nummular eczema. Appearance of fungating tumors of the skin signifies a late stage of the disease. The appearance of plaques may be preceded by a chronic, intractable eczema. Histologically, this neoplasm resembles Hodgkin disease.

Metastatic Carcinoma: Carcinomas rarely metastasize to the skin. When they do appear, they are asymptomatic nodules without much inflammatory infiltrate or a tendency to ulcerate. The overall incidence of skin metastases developing from tumors elsewhere is approximately 3%-4%. The common location for the primary tumor is the female breast, with a somewhat lesser frequency in the gastrointestinal tract, lung, kidney, or uterus. Clinically, metastatic skin tumors show a variable picture with single to multiple lesions that range from small, discrete nodules to thickened plaques. Frequently, the lesions have a definite vascular pattern. Most of them occur in the skin near the site of the primary tumor, although some will preferentially metastasize to the scalp. In metastatic tumors, it is essential to recognize that the skin is secondarily involved and that the primary tumor lies elsewhere.

Cutaneous Manifestations of Internal Diseases

The skin may be part of a generalized disorder of the body as follows:

1. A general metabolic or degenerative disorder may occur in the epidermis or dermis, with reflected disturbed function.
2. The skin may be a passive participant.
3. The skin may be the site of reactions to a disorder that is either generalized or located in some other part of the body, e.g., allergic response.

THE SKIN AS A PARTICIPANT OF GENERALIZED DISEASE

The skin serves as a clue to the general condition of the body, e.g., anemia is reflected in the skin as pallor; dehydration can be assessed by turgor of the skin; lack of adequate nutrition can be assessed by the general appearance and feel of the skin.

Generalized infection: Such diseases as tuberculosis, syphilis, viral exanthema, etc, may involve the skin by an invasion of the organism.

Endocrine: The integrity of the skin is in part determined by hormonal control. For example, thyroid hormone is required for a normal turnover of epidermal cells and, therefore, controls the integrity of the epidermis, growth of hair, and secretion of sebum. It also affects the metabolism of collagen and mucopolysaccharides in the skin. Thus, excesses of thyroid are accompanied by a thin, moist epidermis; thin dermis; and thin, fine hair. Absence or decrease of thyroid hormone is accompanied by decreased sweating, arrested hair growth, an atrophic and hyperkeratotic epidermis, absence of sebum secretion, and the accumulation of mucopolysaccharides in the dermis (myxedema).

Androgens are needed for the normal growth of sebaceous glands and of terminal hair in the characteristically male areas (beard, chest, and extremities). The absence of androgens in the male results in reduced growth of hair and sebaceous glands, whereas an excess of androgens in the female (virilism) is reflected by increased growth of hair and sebaceous glands (acne).

Glucocorticoids are necessary for a normal skin, particularly the production of collagen in the dermis. Excess of this hormone (Cushing disease) is reflected in altered hair growth (hypertrichosis) and in the state of the connective tissue (poor wound healing, purpura, striae). Pituitary hormones very likely affect the skin; with two exceptions, this has not been well defined.

1. Pigmentation (production of melanin) is controlled by both ACTH and melanocyte-stimulating hormone, MSH (hyperpigmentation in Addison disease).
2. Hypersecretion of growth hormone affects the connective tissue of the dermis (acromegaly). One of the signs of acromegaly is excessive dermis, which results in enlargement of the nose, jaws, fingers, and toes.

Other metabolic abnormalities: Vitamin deficiencies are classically associated with altered skin, especially in experimental animals. In man, vitamin A controls keratinization, and in its absence there is hyperkeratosis. Vitamin C protects the integrity of dermal connective tissue and vessels, and in its absence there may be purpura and poor wound healing as well as exuberance of connective tissue in the mucous membranes; some of the B vitamins have been associated with a variety of changes, including eczema and seborrheic dermatitis, but this remains to be proven.

Pellagra is a light-sensitive eruption caused by niacin deficiency.

Porphyrin abnormalities characteristically produce a light-sensitive, vesicular or eczematous eruption in the skin. This response is thought to result from the accumulation or liberation of abnormal porphyrins in the skin which produce toxic effects when exposed to light.

Diabetes is associated with a variety of skin manifestations that may be the direct consequence of a disturbed carbohydrate or lipid metabolism in the skin, leading to a reduced resistance to infection by pyogenic and fungal organisms and disturbances of the vasculature and dermal connective tissue, resulting in necrobiosis lipoidica and pigmented patches.

Collagen diseases (lupus erythematosus, dermatomyositis, scleroderma) are all diseases that affect the dermal connective tissue and vasculature.

Other defects of connective tissue are also manifested in the skin, such as tuberous sclerosis, Ehlers-Danlos syndrome, and pseudoxanthoma elasticum. In addition, the skin commonly participates in a variety of hereditary and chromosomal disorders such as Hurler syndrome, Turner syndrome, mongolism, etc. Certain metabolic reactions result in abnormal by-products or alter enzymatic function in the skin as well as elsewhere. The accumulation of phenylalanine in phenylketonuria specifically inhibits the synthesis of melanin from tyrosine and results in blue eyes, blond hair, and pale skin. The drain of tryptophane into a proliferating carcinoid accompanied by poor diet may result in a deficiency of niacin and produce a pellagra-like syndrome.

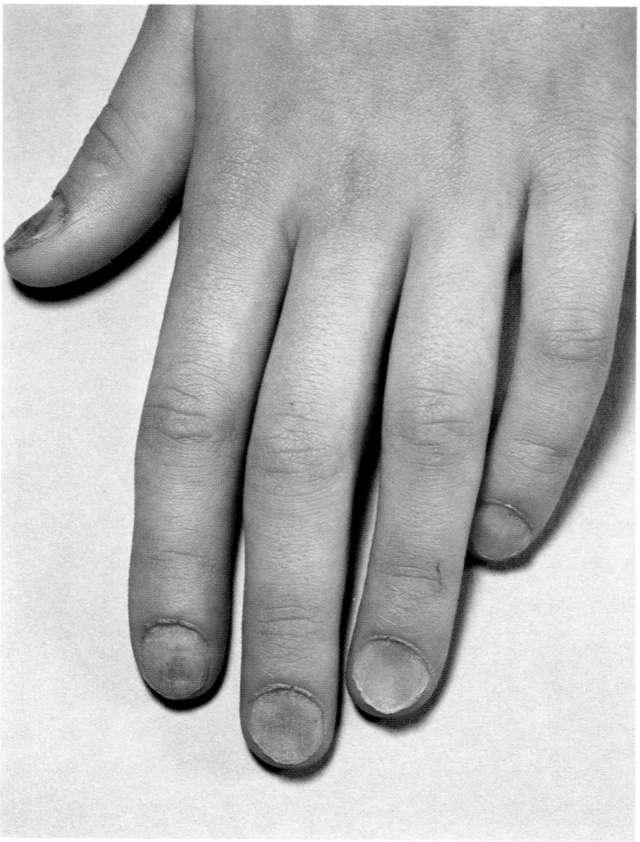

Figure 125. Koilonychia associated with iron deficiency

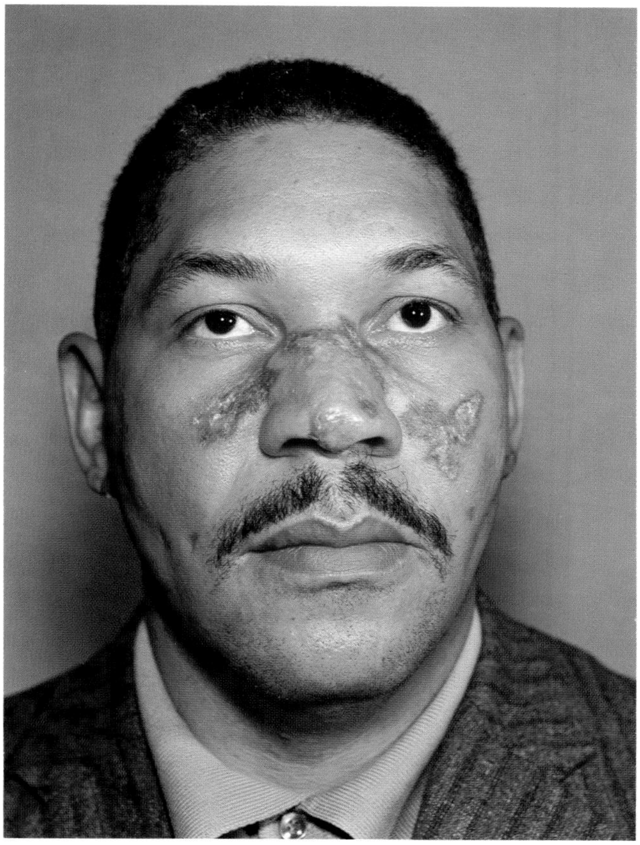

Figure 126. Discoid lupus erythematosus

THE SKIN AS A PASSIVE PARTICIPANT IN GENERALIZED DISORDERS

The skin as a passive participant in generalized disorders is frequently the site of abnormal metabolism. The bilirubin in jaundice, for example, accumulates in the skin, while in alcaptonuria, the protein-complexed polymer of homogentisic acid is deposited as a black pigment in the skin. Uric acid crystals may precipitate into the skin in gout (tophi), and elevations of blood lipids are frequently accompanied by asymptomatic accumulations of lipids in the skin (xanthomatosis).

A variety of allergic reactions and other phenomena

Figure 129. Reiter disease associated with arthritis

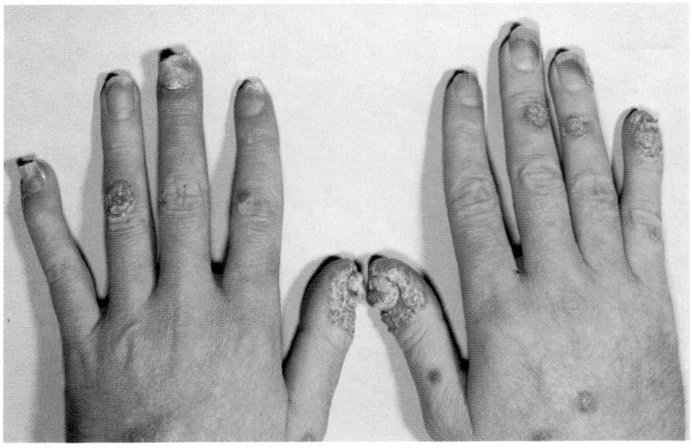

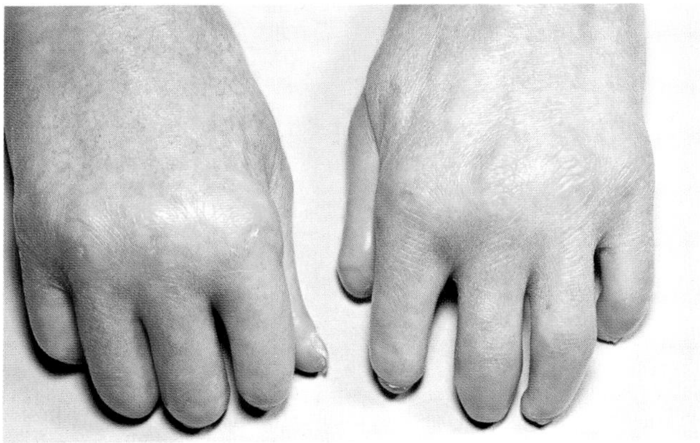

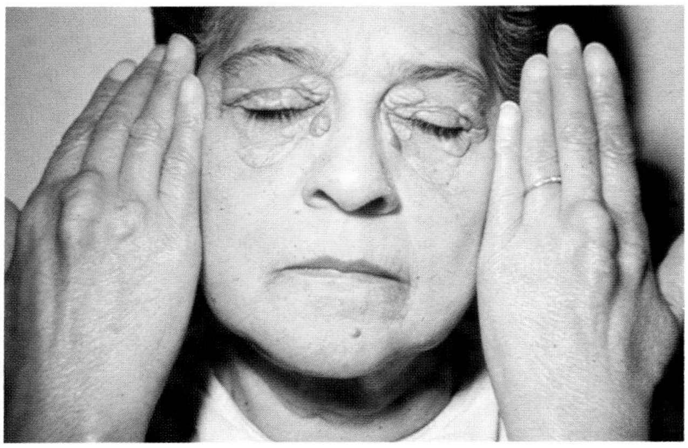

Figure 127. (top) Scleroderma

Figure 128. (bottom) Xanthoma tuberosum

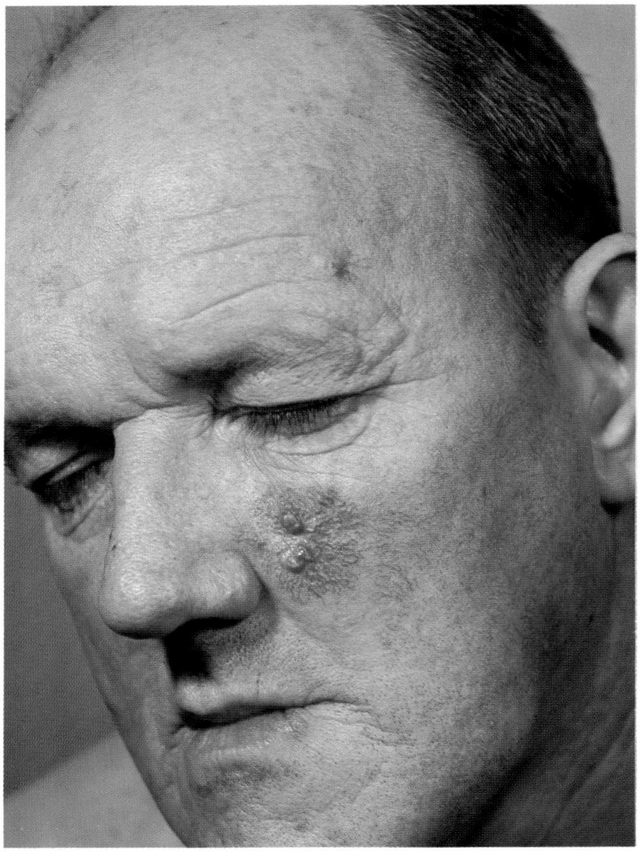

Figure 130. Angiomas associated with cirrhosis of the liver

in the skin may represent a reaction to underlying neoplasm, collagen disorder, infection, etc. In addition, generalized pruritus may be the sign of an underlying lymphoma or undiagnosed uremia. *Dermatomyositis* in adults is associated at least 50% of the time with an underlying malignancy. *Acanthosis nigricans* (a disorder of keratinization) often accompanies underlying malignancy or endocrine disturbances. *Ichthyosis*, a disturbance of keratinization, when not congenital, may accompany underlying lymphoma. *Generalized exfoliative dermatitis* is occasionally caused by disseminated malignancy.

Figure 132. Calcinosis cutis

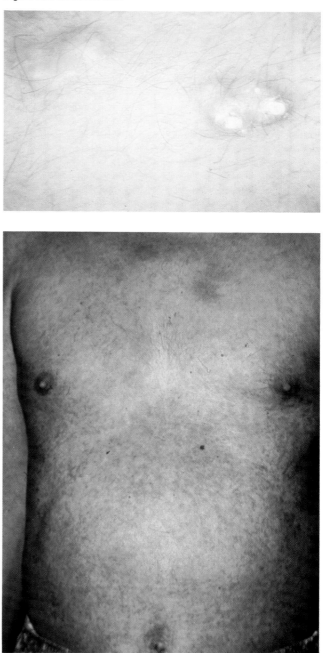

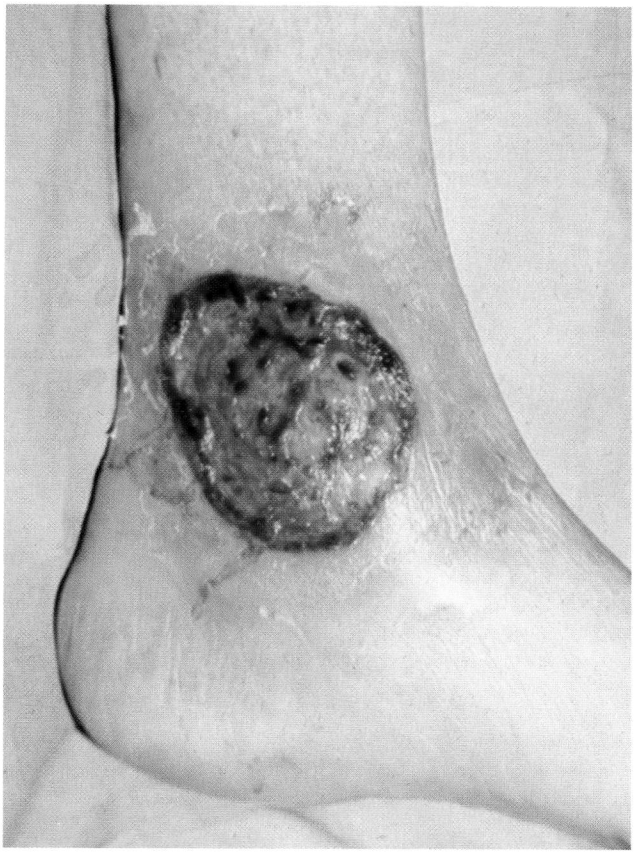

Figure 131. Ulcer of leg associated with polycythemia vera

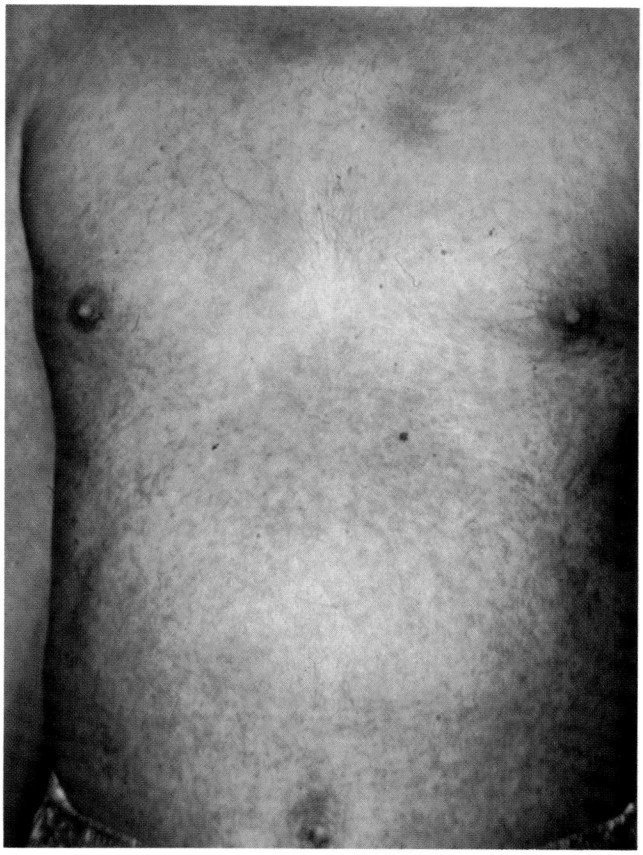

Figure 133. Urticaria pigmentosa

Principles of Topical Treatment

Internal and general medication and environmental control will assume increasing importance in the management of dermatoses; however, it is probable that local and topical therapy will never be entirely abandoned in the treatment of skin diseases. Topical treatment still constitutes the most potent therapeutic weapon in the management of most cutaneous diseases.

For the purposes of topical therapy, lesions may be divided into acute, subacute, and chronic. Generally, baths and wet dressings are used in the acute stage, lotions and pastes in the subacute stage, and ointments and creams in the chronic stage.

TOPICAL CORTICOSTEROID THERAPY

The adjunctive use of topical corticosteroids in the successful management of inflammatory skin lesions has dramatically changed topical therapy. The corticosteroids have gained an unchallenged position in dermatologic therapy.

Topical corticosteroids are effective primarily because of their anti-inflammatory, antipruritic, and vasoconstrictive actions.

The corticosteroids used in topical therapy are called glucocorticoids because of their action on carbohydrate metabolism, thus distinguishing them from mineralocorticoids with their action on salt balance. Although the glucocorticoids are best known for their anti-inflammatory properties, they also possess antiallergic activity.

Corticosteroid creams and ointments have been found to be helpful as adjunctive therapy in all types of eczema including infantile and atopic dermatitis, contact dermatitis, seborrheic dermatitis, pruritus ani, pruritus vulvae, nummular eczema, and exfoliative dermatitis. Other uses for the topical corticosteroid under occlusive dressing are psoriasis, lichen planus (flexural type), lichen simplex chronicus, and granuloma annulare.

TOPICAL TREATMENT OF ACUTE LESIONS

Acute inflammation of the skin is termed acute dermatitis and is characterized by redness, swelling, heat, and itching rather than pain.

The management of acute dermatitis is to soothe the skin and alleviate the patient's discomfort. "*The more angry and acute the eruption, the more mild the remedy*" is a worthwhile rule to follow. Baths, wet dressings, and lotions are used to soothe the skin.

Baths (emulsion colloids)

A soothing colloid bath should be taken once or twice daily. The patient should not remain in the bath long enough to permit the skin to become soggy or macerated.

Starch baths (e.g., Linit starch) or oatmeal baths (e.g., Aveeno or Aveeno Oilated) may be helpful.

Wet Dressings

One of the most useful modalities in dermatologic therapy is the "wet dressing." This type of therapy

- is an efficacious means of cleansing the skin of adherent crusts and debris.
- constitutes an excellent measure for maintaining drainage of infected areas.
- is an effective vehicle for local application of heat or cold.
- can be used to macerate the skin surface and thus effect keratolytic action.
- prevents rapid changes of temperature at skin surface—thus provides an excellent antipruritic action.
- acts as a soothing agent and is among the most-effective therapy for relieving inflammation.
- tends to open blisters and helps bring medication to the bases of eroded or ulcerated areas.

Solutions used: Many solutions for wet dressings can be used. The two most efficacious in the author's opinion are: Liquid aluminum acetate (Burow Solution, N.F.) diluted with 20-30 parts of water, and Alibour solution for infected dermatitis (0.6 gm copper sulfate, 2.0 gm zinc sulfate, 100.0 ml camphor water as dilute 1:20).

SUBACUTE LESIONS

Lotions

The application of wet dressings is a laborious task, requires patience, and is not to be employed any longer than is necessary. In the subacute stage with its dry, crusted, scaly areas, the best treatment is with lotions. These offer a cleaner and more satisfactory form of treatment, are more easily applied, and do not require bandaging. A lotion is a liquid suspension containing finely divided particles for application to the skin.

Lotions usually should not have over 40% powder and not over 10% glycerine. The addition of 1% bentonite will keep the solution in suspension. The physician can add bentonite and Iron Oxide, N.F., for coloring:

1. Zinc oxide — 20.0 gm

Zinc oxide		20.0 gm
Talc	aa	20.0 gm
Glycerin		6.0 gm
Aqua	qs	120 ml

2. Calamine lotion (note that calamine, which is basically zinc oxide, has replaced talc):

Calamine		20.0 gm
Zinc oxide		20.0 gm
Glycerin		6.0 gm
Aqua calcis	qs	120 ml

3. Boric acid can be added for antisepsis; the addition of bentonite will keep the solution in suspension.
4. Starch lotion is often indicated for inflammatory conditions of the skin.

Antipruritics may be added to lotions in the following percents:

Menthol	0.25%–0.5%
Phenol	0.5%– 1%
Liq. carbonis detergens	3%– 10%
Salicylic acid	1%– 2%
Ichthammol	3%– 10%
Chloral hydrate	2%– 5%
Spirits of camphor	2%– 4%

Antipruritics that may be added to calamine lotion are as follows:

Menthol		0.3 gm
Phenol		0.6 gm
Coal tar solution		10 ml
Calamine lotion	qs	120 ml

If the above lotions are too drying, 50% of an oil can be substituted for the vehicle to make a liniment. For example, olive oil can replace the glycerin in calamine lotion to make a liniment.

Pastes

Pastes differ from ointments in that they contain 50% powder, whereas ointments may consist of 100% oil base.

With pastes we may incorporate ichthammol (3%), naftalan (5%–10%), and crude coal tar (5%).

CHRONIC LESIONS

Ointments

From the acute and subacute stages, we now enter the chronic stage, and it is often advantageous to work up from thin ointments to ointments of a thick consistency. A bland ointment may contain an aquaphor or aqua rosae base.

This is a pleasant mixture that can be readily dispensed anywhere. Occasionally, a heavier paste may be preferred, and zinc paste in varying proportions can be prescribed.

Inflammatory lesions of practically any type will respond to glucocorticosteroids.

A major development in the use of topical steroids was the observation that occlusion of a diseased area treated with one of the glucorticosteroids greatly enhanced the therapeutic potential of the given steroid. A polyethylene plastic film (e.g., Saran wrap) was used for the original occlusive dressings, but any material that offers a barrier to water and heat loss will produce similar effects.

There are many topical steroids available depending on the percentage of glucocorticoid activity desired and the type of base required, i.e., cream, ointment, or lotion.

In chronic or more torpid and thickened areas, the following drugs are often prescribed for their stimulating effect:

1.	Oil of cade	5%–15% ointment or paste
2.	Oil of rusci	5%–15% ointment or paste
3.	Crude coal tar	5%–20% ointment or paste (may be used in full strength)
4.	Resorcin	4%–10% in ointment or paste
5.	Salicylic acid	4%–10% in ointment or paste
6.	Sulfur	4%–10% in ointment or paste
7.	Amm. mercury	5%–10% in ointment or paste
8.	Chrysarobin	4%–10% in ointment or paste
9.	Lenigallol	1%–10% in ointment or paste
10.	Cignolin	0.1%– 1% in ointment or paste

Dry, chronic, thickened, lichenfied, scratched eczema offers the most difficult problem, and tasks the skill of the physician. The remedies employed are all reducing agents and, of these, tar is outstanding. Salicylic acid 3%–5% may be most suitable if the lesion is scaly.

Oil-in-water ointments

Hydrophilic ointment U.S.P. is the base used for most moist surfaces. The type of preparation is not recommended as a good occlusive agent.

Water-in-oil ointments

Water-in-oil preparations are used primarily for dry, keratotic surfaces. They are occlusive and have good emollient properties.

Glossary

Atrophy: Loss of tissue substance discernible as a depressed lesion. Fibrosis frequently accompanies atrophy but is not a necessary process in atrophy.
Auspitz sign: Punctate bleeding seen when the scales are removed from a lesion. This is noted primarily in psoriasis in which the suprapapillary plate is thin.
Café au lait: Light-brown spots on an otherwise normal skin, usually caused by von Recklinghausen disease.
Darier sign: Wheal formation when the lesion is stroked, the wheal being most visible in the lesion. This localization of the wheal is best seen in the childhood type of urticaria pigmentosa.
Dermographism and white dermographism: *Dermographism* is an exaggerated normal triple response of Lewis. *White dermographism* is a paradoxical response to stroking of the skin in which vasodilation (normal response) is absent and is replaced by actual vasoconstriction.
Erythema, telangiectasia, and angioma: *Erythema* is defined as a temporary vasodilatation in the skin. *Telangiectasia* is defined as a permanent vasodilatation in the skin. The cutoff point in time is not defined, and the terms may be used loosely in prolonged vasodilatation without a definitive diagnosis. *Angioma* is vasodilatation of large numbers of newly formed vessels.
"id": A skin rash associated with but in a distant location from the main infection; when the infection is removed the 'id' disappears.
Intertriginous: Chafe of the skin occurring frequently on opposed surfaces; also erythema or eczema of chafed skin.
Lichenification: Thickening of the skin with accentuation of the surface markings. Lichenification implies that there exists an increase in the thickness of the epidermis (acanthosis) and intercellular fluid accumulation (spongiosis).
Nikolsky sign: The enlargement of a blister laterally by light pressure on the blister. It is used generally in the easy removal of the epidermis by gentle pressure of the finger on the skin laterally to produce a sheering force in the epidermis.
Oil of cade: Juniper tar in an oil vehicle.
Onychia: Inflammation of the nail bed resulting in loss of the nail.
Papulosquamous eruption: Raised lesions with scales. For the purpose of differential diagnosis, all eruptions of this type are considered in the papulosquamous reaction pattern, even those with specific etiologic agents. Most textbooks, however, cover only a portion of the papulosquamous diseases.
Paronychia: Inflammation in the folds of tissue around the fingernails.
Perlèche: Thickening and desquamation of the epithelium of the lips, usually resulting from oral moniliasis, common in children.
Photosensitivity: Reaction of the skin sensitive to light.
Poikiloderma: A mottled appearance of the skin due to pigmentary changes and atrophy. Both atrophy and telangiectasia may be minimal, although both are usually found.
Pustule: A small blister on the skin, filled with pus.
Scales and keratoses: *Scales* are thin sheets of stratum corneum and, even when the total thickness is great, their lamellar structure is apparent. *Keratoses* are horny accumulations of stratum corneum with fusion of the sheets of stratum corneum into a unit mass.
Serpiginous: Creeping from part to part, snake-like.
Sulfurated lime: A mixture of at least 60% calcium sulfide with various proportions of calcium sulfate and carbon. Useful as a depilatory and in skin and pustular diseases.
Torpid: Lacking in normal vigor and facility.
Trichotillomania: A morbid impulse to pull out one's own hair.
Verrucous: Warty; covered with warts.
Vitiligo: Failure of the skin to form melanin, leaving patches of depigmentations which tend to enlarge.

Upjohn